TEXAS HOLD 'EM POKER

BEGIN AND WIN

Paul Mendelson

RIGHT WAY

Typeset in 11pt Times New Roman by Letterpart Ltd., Reigate, Surrey.

Printed and bound in Great Britain by Cox & Wyman Ltd., Reading, Berkshire.

The *Right Way* series is published by Elliot Right Way Books, Brighton Road, Lower Kingswood, Tadworth, Surrey, KT20 6TD, U.K. For information about our company and the other books we publish, visit our website at www.right-way.co.uk

TEXAS HOLD 'EM POKER

By the same author

Bridge For Complete Beginners
The Right Way To Play Bridge
Bridge: Play Your Cards Right
Control The Bidding

Uniform with this book

CONTENTS

1. **Introduction to Poker** 9
    Universal Ranking of Poker Hands 10

2. **Texas Hold 'Em Poker** 15
    Introduction 15
    Working Through the Game 20
    Further Hold 'Em Etiquette and Rules 28
    Betting 31
    Showdowns 32
    Forms of Game 33
    The Buy-In 34
    Betting Limits 35
    Tournaments 37

3. **Basic Strategy for Cash Games** 39
    Patience, Patience, Patience 39
    On "Tilt" 40
    Starting Hands 41
    Hands Not to Play 43
    Suited Connectors 43
    Position 44
    On the Button 45
    Calling or Raising? 46
    How Much to Raise? 47
    Action on the Flop 49
    Raising to Save Money (or as a Semi-Bluff) 57
    Holding the Nuts 58
    Action on the Turn and River 60
    Betting on the River 62
    Check-Raise 63

Behaviour and Emotions 63
Recommended Starting Hands for Cash
Games 65

4. **Tournaments** 67
How a Tournament Works 67
Tactics 70
Early in the Tournament 70
In Mid-Tournament 71
Chip and a Chair 73
Short-Stacking 73
Pot Odds 74
Towards the End 74
Chip Counts and Other Pressure Plays 75
The Final Table 76
Short-Handed Games and Heads Up 77
Tournament Starting Hands 77
Late Position Calling 80

5. **Tells** 81
How to Behave at the Poker Table 82
Key Tells 83
"Putting" an Opponent on a Hand 86
Bad Beat Stories 87

6. **Percentages and Odds: Understanding Your**
Chances 91
Using Pot Odds and Drawing Odds 93
Implied Pot Odds 94
"Pot Committed" 96

7. **Bankroll and Money Management** 99
Setting Your Bankroll 100
Choosing Your Game 100
Coming and Going 102

House Rakes and Charges 102
Tipping 103

8. **Online Poker** 105
Play Money or Real Money? 105
Which Site? 106
Getting Started 106
Making Character Notes 107
Sit Over Weakness 109
Steal Blinds Aggressively 110
Bluffing 110

9. **Top Ten Tips for Texas Hold 'Em** 111

Glossary 119

Index 126

1

INTRODUCTION TO POKER

Card games have been played for centuries. Hours of excitement and fascination have been spent in plush salons, sleazy basement dives and friendly home games and, most importantly for poker, above all other games, fortunes have been won and lost.

In 1837, poker developed into, more or less, the game we have now. Previously, a short deck – or pack – of only twenty cards was utilized, but with the advent of the 52-card deck, which we know today, the game changed dramatically and for the better.

Since then, all poker games have been based on the purest form of the game: *5-Card Stud*. In this version, each player is dealt five cards and the betting begins, players having a chance to bet that theirs is the best hand at the table. Mostly, players fold – throw away their cards – and wait for a better hand. If one player bets more money into the pot than anyone is prepared to match, he takes the pot whether he really has the strongest hand or not; he doesn't even have to show his cards. If one or more of the other players match the highest bet, there is a showdown – where all those players show their cards and the player with the best hand takes the spoils.

All poker hands, in every form of the game there is, have a ranking. It is how you tell who has the best hand. It is arranged in order based purely on the statistical probability of such a hand occurring, from the best hand and least likely to occur – the Royal Flush – to the worst hand and most commonly seen type of hand, containing nothing but a High Card.

UNIVERSAL RANKING OF POKER HANDS

Hand	Explanation	Example
Royal Flush	AKQJ10 in the same suit	A♥ K♥ Q♥ J♥ 10♥
Straight Flush	5 same-suit cards in sequence	8♠ 7♠ 6♠ 5♠ 4♠
4 of a Kind	all 4 cards of the same rank	K♠ K♥ K♦ K♣ ⊠
Full House	3 of a Kind and a Pair	A♠ A♥ A♦ 5♦ 5♠
Flush	5 cards of the same suit	Q♦ 10♦ 6♦ 4♦ 2♦
Straight	any 5 cards in sequence	J♥ 10♠ 9♥ 8♦ 7♣
3 of a Kind	3 cards of the same rank	7♥ 7♦ 7♠ ⊠ ⊠
2 Pair	2 x 2 cards of the same rank	Q♥ Q♣ 3♠ 3♥ ⊠
1 Pair	2 cards of the same rank	K♥ K♦ ⊠ ⊠ ⊠
High Card	no hand, but highest card held	A♦ ⊠ ⊠ ⊠ ⊠

⊠ = any other, non matching, card

All poker games are based on this ranking and all poker hands are made up of five cards. In some versions of the game, more than five cards are dealt to each player, or are available for use. However, only five cards can be used to form a poker hand. Never more; never less.

5-Card Stud Poker is mostly about psychology, guts and the ability to mask your real emotions. You got your five cards and that was it. You had to fold them, pretend that you had the best hand or, if you really did have a great hand, pretend that you didn't have one to lure other players into the betting action. But players wanted more action, more of a chance to stay involved in the hand. The solution was a development that, once again, was to change the face of poker: The Draw.

5-Card Draw was similar to Stud Poker but with a crucial twist. After the five cards had been dealt, there would be a round of betting. Then, each player in turn could exchange one or more of the cards in his hand, for new cards from the deck, to try to improve his hand. Then there would be a further round of betting. The result was that players made better hands and there was twice the opportunity for betting, meaning twice the opportunity to try to bluff, bully or seduce your opponents. Some players consider 5-Card Draw Poker the purest form of the game, but it is nowhere near as popular as many other versions.

As the third millennium dawned, the popularity of poker was beginning to expand from the millions who played it regularly in the USA, to hundreds of millions throughout the world. Inspired by television coverage, featuring secret cameras which revealed the players' cards to the audience, the huge sums of money at stake for the most subtle of decisions and the sheer human drama of the game, poker's universal charm became irresistible. Moreover, the Internet became the preferred venue for playing, especially amongst those starting out in the game. The ability to practise anonymously, to enter free tournaments and to play against really good players from all over the world, without leaving home, has become a fine alternative to watching mindless television or sitting in gridlocked traffic.

In the twenty-first century, there is an abundance of different poker games: 5-Card Stud and Draw, 7-Card Stud, Hi/Low variations, Omaha and, the "Cadillac of poker games", *Texas Hold 'Em*. There are also the many home-spun variations with jokers, wild cards, strange betting rules and topsy-turvey last-minute turnarounds. However, most poker players in the world today favour Texas Hold 'Em. It's the version which best combines skill with luck, which involves just the right amount of action, and the one which produces the most excitement right down to the very last card. That's why this book focuses on Texas Hold 'Em.

The way you keep score in poker is with the chips in front of you. The chips represent money. In a cash game, you might buy $500 worth of chips and sit down at a table with them. You might get up again two hours, six hours, twelve hours later, with ten times your original stake, or you might stumble from the table shell-shocked and dazed, with nothing.

Since the 1990s, tournament poker has become hugely popular, both in card rooms and on the Internet. You pay an entry fee – say $50 – and you receive chips to the value of, say, 1,000 units, as does everyone else. You then play until, one by one, players go bust and get knocked out, until finally, from a field of players which might have numbered twenty, a hundred or even as many as ten thousand, there is just one table of ten players left with everybody else's chips divided up amongst them. This *Final Table* is a destination all tournament players dream about reaching, as here you are guaranteed a substantial prize and you are still in the hunt to win the whole event. These ten players continue playing until only one is left.

Usually, in a tournament, the winner will receive between one quarter and one third of all the entry fees. In the World Championships – the World Series of Poker (WSOP) – played annually in Las Vegas each May and June, that first prize passed one million dollars years ago. Now, the winner is expected to take home in excess of five million dollars. To do it he, or she, has to beat several thousand of the world's best players. In the good old days, only the hardened old pros stood a chance. Now, their places are being usurped by young players, from all over the world, who have learnt at their computers and are coming to gun for the professionals. Two have already won the WSOP in the twenty-first century, and their challenge is going to grow and grow.

At home, you can play for pennies or stakes much more substantial. In casinos and card rooms, there are modest games available. In the Internet card rooms, you can play for no stake at all, although, because there is no money at stake, the betting is wild and the game barely resembles poker. Or you can join in big cash games and in tournaments with entry fees from $5 to $1,200 and probably bigger ones too. Wherever you choose to play, however, one thing is certain. Once you see what an amazing game poker can be, you will be spoilt for all other card games. No other game provides the cerebral stimulation and the roller-coaster emotional ride as poker.

Start to play now. Expect to spend months or years learning the game – which is pleasurable if, sometimes, a little expensive – and then prepare to crush your opponents, outwit your friends, bluff your bosses and haul in the pot. Nothing, you will find, beats that exquisite moment when you, metaphorically or literally, reach across the table, open your arms around that volcano-style pile of chips, and draw them all towards you, because you, yes you, have just won all the chips. There really isn't any need to smile, to gloat, to celebrate (although feel free if you so wish), just knowing that the other players are watching you and those chips – their chips – and they are all yours. That's quite a feeling.

A few pieces of business before we get going. Firstly, when referring to your poker opponents in this book, I call them "he". It's true that poker used to be utterly male dominated, but there are now millions of women players and it won't be long before one of them becomes world champion. I simply use "he" because it saves a keystroke every time and, like all poker players, when I'm not playing, I'm lazy!

Secondly, when talking about stakes, I use dollars. Obviously, you'll play with whatever currency is relevant to your game. Online poker rooms usually offer a choice of currencies in which you can play. Because, to my mind, poker is the quintessential American game, and I've played almost all my live poker in Las Vegas, I always think of bets in dollars.

Finally, poker is a game. A serious one to be sure, but a game nonetheless. Sometimes, it's easy to forget that – and because you will have momentous ups and vertiginous downs, I strongly recommend that you keep it to the forefront of your mind at all times.

2

TEXAS HOLD 'EM POKER

Introduction

Texas Hold 'Em is the Rolls Royce or Cadillac of poker games. It is the form favoured by the professional players and it is the one which features every year in the five-day marathon which is the climax to the WSOP – the World Championships – or the "Big One", as it is often called. Thankfully, it is incredibly easy to learn which means that you will be playing before you know it.

Firstly, let's look at the briefest of descriptions – and then we'll explore the game, the terminology, and the ritual in more detail.

In a game of Texas Hold 'Em, each player is dealt, face down, two *hole cards* – so-called because the cards are "in the hole", in the dark to the other players, hidden – which he looks at without showing them to his opponents. These are his cards and only his. There is now a round of betting based on the strength of those two cards alone.

Next, three cards are dealt face up in the middle of the table. This is known as *the flop*. These three cards are community cards, which can be used by all of the players, together with their two hidden cards, to make up a 5-card poker hand. There is another round of betting.

Now, a fourth community card is turned over and added to flop. This is known as *the turn* or *fourth street*. Another round of betting follows, before the final card is dealt, face up, in the middle of the table. This final card is known as *the river*, or *fifth street*. It is so-called because it is often the river on which a player's dreams go floating away when his opponent's hand is suddenly transformed by the arrival of the final card.

There is now one final round of betting in which the remaining players use one or both of their own cards, plus any of the five community cards on the table, to make up the best 5-card poker hand. If more than one player believes that he holds the best hand, there will be a *showdown*, in which the players will show their hidden cards and announce their hand.

The winner takes all.

It is possible, although very rare, that the five cards on the table form the best possible hand and, if that is the case, all the remaining players would share the pot between them.

Let's look at a quick example:

Player A holds   A♣ 7♣

Player B holds   K♠ Q♠

Player C holds   J♦ J♥

There is a round of betting, based on just these hole cards during which strong hands may raise the betting and drive out players who hold weaker hands. Once the betting is complete, the flop is dealt:

The flop comes

All three players will feel that they have quite a good hand now.

Player A has a Pair of aces – that is pretty strong.

Player B has no hand yet but if a 10 were to appear, he would hold the highest possible Straight – what we would call the "Nut Straight".

Player C is winning right now, holding a powerful 3 of a Kind jacks.

There is a second round of betting. Player A might well put in a bet, believing his Pair of aces to be the best hand. Player B might give up, since he doesn't have a made hand yet. Player C would certainly call the bet and might even raise the betting, since he is virtually sure that his hand is the best right now.

However, let's assume that all the players stay in the hand and watch what happens.

The fourth community card, or turn, is now dealt:

The 8♠ has not changed the situation much, except that Player B, whilst still holding no hand, has now developed an extra chance of winning. Not only would a 10 give him the Nut Straight, but another spade would give him the highest possible Flush – the Nut Flush – since A♠ is on the board and he holds the next highest spade: K♠. So, while Player C is currently winning, with Player A in second place, Player B could overtake both of them if and when the fifth and final card is dealt.

Assuming, perhaps unrealistically, that the betting fails to drive out any of the players and they are all still in the hand, here comes the fifth and final community card – the river.

This is a big card for everyone. For Player A, it gives him 2 Pair – aces and 7s; for Player B, he has now made the best possible Flush – the table shows A♠ and he holds K♠: no one can have a higher value Flush than him – whilst Player C still holds three jacks, which still looks a strong hand.

There is now a final round of betting and, with each player holding what appears to be a good hand, there could be some big bets made. If the players end up having to show their hands, it will be Player B who will be smiling – he will collect all the chips. Players A and C will not be happy. They had good hands, but having the second or third best hand at poker is the worst situation of all because, in a showdown, you never win anything for being second best.

In a real game, the action might not have reached those final stages because Player C, holding the best hand until the very last card appeared, might have chosen to raise the betting so high that neither Player A nor B may have felt it worthwhile to stay in the hand. In that case, Player C would have won the pot at an earlier stage.

Here, then, is the classic poker dilemma. When you hold what you think is the best hand, do you bet it strongly, telling everyone you are strong, and risk all the other players giving up and you winning only a small amount of money?

Or, do you feign indifference, keep all the other players in the hand and then hope to surprise them at the end and lure them into betting more than they should?

That is one of the hardest, most skilful decisions in the game. Represent strength and risk winning little; slow play a good hand in an attempt to win more, but risk another hand overtaking you (as Hand B did) and then lose everything at a later stage?

To answer briefly: if you're starting out at poker, when you have the best hand put in a big bet. It is definitely better to win something than to get outdrawn – have a player make a better hand than you because perfect cards appear for him on the flop, turn, or river – and outplayed later and lose everything. As you gain in knowledge and experience, you can modify that action.

There is a further scenario however, unique to poker. You may have a very poor hand, but choose to bluff your way into winning a pot. If you bet aggressively and confidently, other players may believe that you have the best hand at the table, and they may all concede to you. Most players will tell you that it is far more satisfying to win a pot with a bluff than to have the best hand and just get paid what you feel you were owed. Without the aspect of bluffing, poker would be a very dull game, since the best hand would always win the money. Bluffing changes everything.

In order to understand the game and its terms and rituals, we will now play out another hand, more slowly, introducing each part of the action. You do not have to remember any of this since, as it will happen each and every hand you deal, it will become second nature within a couple of hours of play. Following this example, we'll look at some important rules and tactics, some money management skills, tournament tips and ideas for Internet games. To conclude, there are ten vital tips for you to take to your first game: remember these, and you will be off to a great start.

Working Through the Game

The ideal number for a game of poker is probably between five and eight players, but tables often hold ten players, and just two people playing "head to head" can be breathtakingly exciting. Home games have been played on kitchen tables for centuries, so throw a piece of green baize (or some felt, a rug, a carpet, even a towel) over your table and we can begin – almost.

Get hold of a full deck of cards, take out the jokers and give the pack a good shuffle.

You are going to need some *chips*. You can buy these easily over the Internet or from shops. You can use pennies, or play for cash or even, when following these pages, use matchsticks or sweets or ball-bearings. But remember, when the game really starts, you will be playing to win or to lose. You don't get to collect your chips back again at the end of the evening and laugh about what good fun it all was. The chips are your money, and you must play to win. So, give each player about thirty chips, and that will do for the moment.

Now, a word about the *dealer*:

Dealing is either performed by a staff member provided by a card club or casino, or it is done by the players themselves. This might be done by drawing for seats: everyone chooses a card; the player with the highest is the dealer, the next highest on his right, and so on. If the players perform this task, the first person shuffles the deck thoroughly, asks the player on his right to cut the deck and then deals the hand. Then the role passes to the next player, in a clockwise rotation. If there is an appointed dealer, then there will be a "dealer button" (a white plastic disc with "dealer" printed on it) placed in front of the player to indicate for whom the cards are being dealt.

At poker, everything moves clockwise from the dealer. At Hold 'Em, your position at the table in relation to the dealer is absolutely crucial. As you will learn, to be the dealer can be very advantageous – that is why the role must move around the table after each hand.

The dealer shuffles the cards and offers them to his right-hand opponent who lifts off a portion of the deck and places it face down next to the remaining cards. The dealer then puts the remaining cards on top of the portion cut off. This is called the "cut" and it ensures that the dealer hasn't stacked the deck in his favour. Before the dealer begins to distribute the cards, there is still one task to be undertaken.

The player to the left of the dealer must make a *Small Blind* bet, let's say one chip, and the player to his left must make a *Big Blind* bet – usually double the amount of the small bet – two chips. These bets are called the *Blinds* (because you have to make the bet "blind" – without having seen your cards) and they are used to get the action going. You'll see how in a moment. So, with the Blinds placed, the dealer deals one card to each player starting on his left and going around the table. He then deals a second card to each player and stops.

The players look at their cards, ensuring that their opponents cannot see them or the player's reaction to them. There is now a round of betting, based on the strength of these two *hole cards*.

Now, the purpose of the Blind bets becomes clear. If players wish to stay in the hand, they must match – or exceed – the bet placed by the Big Blind (in this example, betting two chips).

This is a key part of poker betting. To stay in the hand, you must match (or, if you think you have the best hand, exceed – by raising) the largest bet currently made. If you choose not to do this, then you must fold (or muck) your cards, discarding them face down in the direction of the dealer. You now take no further part in this particular hand.

If you are down to your last few chips, you may continue in the hand provided that you bet all your chips – known as going "all-in". You cannot be knocked out of the hand because you cannot match the bet, but you must commit every last one of your remaining chips.

At Hold 'Em the strength of the first two cards is quite significant for, reasonably often, the player with the best starting hand ends up being triumphant. Since there are only two cards for each player to see, the best hand available so far would be a Pair – and a Pair of aces would be the highest Pair, and currently, best hand possible. Two low cards of different suits, say 7♣ and 2♦, would be the very worst hand, worth nothing now and unlikely to turn into anything exciting as the game proceeds. We will look at which hands are good and worth playing, and which are not, a little later.

For this round only, the action starts with the player to the left of the Big Blind since the Blinds are deemed to have made a bet already (subsequently, the player to the left of the dealer – the Small Blind bettor – always starts the betting action). Each player in turn must either take one of the following actions, which he says aloud when he is about to do it.

Fold, or *Pass*   This means refusing to bet and throwing away your cards – face down – and taking no further part in the hand. This you would do if you felt that your two cards were not strong enough to continue playing. It is, at this stage, the action you will take most often.

Call   This means that you place a bet exactly matching the current largest bet that has been placed on this round of the betting, in this case, the two chips placed by the Big Blind.

Raise   This is the strongest manoeuvre and means that you are raising the level of the betting to a new high. The minimum by which you can raise the betting will be the same amount as the Big Blind (in this case two chips). In order for other players to remain in the hand, they must now call or re-raise your bet. If you raised by the minimum, your bet would now be four chips.

If all subsequent players fold their hands, you win the pot and you do not need to show your cards. If a player or players match your bet, the hand continues.

Re-Raise   This is another raise on top of an
                       original raise and is a very, very
                       strong move. This might happen if
                       two or more players feel they have
                       premium hands and they want either
                       to increase the size of the pot or to
                       attempt to drive other players out of
                       the action even before it has started.
                       For example, your hole cards might
                       be QQ but you are afraid that if the
                       community cards include an ace or a
                       king, another player might gain a
                       better hand than you. By re-raising,
                       you might make those other players
                       give up before any community cards
                       have appeared.

When the betting reaches the Blind bettors, their actions
are slightly different. If no raises have occurred, the Small
Blind bettor may call for just one chip (he already has one
chip in the pot as his Blind). He can also raise or, if
holding a weak hand, fold.

The Big Blind bettor may, if there have been no raises,
just "check" – see below – as he already has two chips in
the pot. However, he also has the option to raise if he
wishes.

Both Blinds retain the option to fold, call or re-raise if
any player has raised before them.

Check   means that you have already matched
                       the current highest bet on this round of
                       the betting (on subsequent rounds, this
                       includes when no bet has been made
                       by anyone) and you do not, at this
                       point, wish to add anything to the pot.

The game only continues when all players have either folded, or matched the highest bet on the table. If no one calls and the Small Blind folds, the Big Blind wins the three chips without needing to show his hand. The betting might end up with everyone betting two chips, or it may mean that one player has bet ten chips and just one other has called that bet and placed ten chips on the table.

Let's imagine that two players have done that. The chips, which up until now, have been pushed forward by the players in front of them in little piles, get placed – or tossed – into one big pile in the middle of the table. This is *the pot* – the prize for which all the players remaining in the hand are now competing.

(It is important not to throw – or splash – your chips into the middle when you first bet since that will make it difficult for everyone to check that you have bet what you say you have. That is why you push your chips tidily forward in front of you first and then, once that round of betting is complete, everyone then puts their chips into the pot.)

Player A holds

Player B holds

Both are strong hands, but Player A is winning so far since he holds a Pair and Player B holds only a High Card.

The dealer *burns* the top card off the deck (that is to say, he discards the top card face down) and then deals the next three cards in a row into the middle of the table, face-up – this is the flop.

Player A will be sorry to see that ace *on the board* (the community cards that are face up on the table) since his Pair of kings may now be beaten if Player B holds an ace in his hand. As you can see, that is the case. Player B now does hold a Pair of aces and he is beating Player A.

Being to the left of the dealer means that Player A must bet first and he decides to make a bet to see if Player B stays in the hand. In this way, he is testing to see if Player B has been pleased by the appearance of the ace on the table. Player A bets ten chips. Player B now suspects that he has the best hand and he now has a choice of actions. He could simply call the bet (placing ten chips on the table), giving the impression that he wants to stay in the hand but that he is not sure who has the best cards or, he could raise the bet, say to 20 chips, to state clearly that he believes that he has the best hand.

Let's say that he takes the former option and just calls the bet. Each player moves his ten chips into the middle, adding to the pot. The dealer burns the next card and then turns over the following one. The board now shows:

Player A is still not sure that he holds the best hand so, perhaps this time, he checks (indicating that, at the moment, he doesn't want to make a bet). Player B may decide that, with two spades on the board, there is a slight chance that Player A might have two spades in his hand and be on the verge of making a Flush, so he decides to *Bet*.

Bet   is when you are the first player after the flop, turn or river, to make a bet.

Let's say he bets 20 chips. Hand A is now feeling a bit depressed. His two kings were almost certainly the best hand until the ace appeared on the flop but now Player B's confident betting is strongly suggesting that he holds an ace and has the best hand with a Pair of aces.

If Player A continues in this hand, unless another king appears (giving him 3 of a Kind kings – sometimes called *Trips*, so here *Trip kings*) he will lose. Since there are only two kings left in the deck (or held by Player B) out of 46 possible cards (the pack of 52 cards minus Player B's hole cards and minus the four cards on the board), this is very unlikely.

(Take cover: here are some statistics – there is only a 1/23 or 4.3% chance of a third king appearing.)

Therefore, if Player A can work out that Player B really does have a Pair of aces, he should give up on the hand now and fold. He started with the best hand, but the community cards gave his opponent a better hand. Assuming that Player A is good enough to fold such a nice hand as KK, he will throw his cards away and concede. Player B will gather up the pot without having to show his cards (and, almost always, he should not show his cards as the best strategy is to keep your opponents guessing at all times).

Beginners often whine at the end of the hand and ask you to tell them what you actually held. Do not tell them. That is the game of poker: if you want to know what your opponents held, you have to pay to see the cards!

So, the hand doesn't always proceed as far as the river. More often than not, one player makes a bet that is so big, so convincing, that all the other players feel that it is not worthwhile to continue in the hand, and they fold. Of course, in the previous example, Player B really did have the best hand and would probably have still had the best hand even after all five community cards had been dealt.

But, what if he had held almost nothing? He could have bet in the same way, Player A might have reacted in the same way, and Player B might have taken the pot without having any kind of decent hand. That is the beauty of poker. You do not have to have the best hand to win (unless there is a showdown, when you do). If you can convince your opponents that you have the best hand, then they may all fold, and you may win the pot without ever having to show your cards. That can be an amazing feeling.

Incidentally, should the deal have proceeded further, the dealer would, again, have burnt the top card and dealt the final community card – the river – face up onto the table. The dealer's job is now done and he can relax and watch the hand played to its conclusion.

Further Hold 'Em Etiquette and Rules

Aces High

With the exception of a Straight, aces are always high. In a Straight, they can be both high and low. A High Straight (A K Q J 10) is the best Straight available, the so-called *Nut Straight*, but an ace can also be low in a low Straight (A 2 3 4 5) sometimes called the *Wheel* or *Bicycle*. Although the ace is involved in this low Straight, the highest card is the five, and that means that, if someone held 2 3 4 5 6, that would beat the five-high Straight.

The Nuts   means the best hand available based on the community cards showing. A Nut Straight would be the highest Straight available; the Nut Flush, the highest possible Flush.

Kickers

At poker, when two players have hands of matching ranks, the height of the cards is key. So, if two players hold 3 of a Kind, the player holding KKK will beat the player holding 888.

The size of the other cards in the hand may also become important in the matter of *Kickers*. A kicker is the next highest card not involved in the formation of a poker hand combination. For example, if two players held the following hands, it would be the kicker which decides who wins the hand:

Player A   8 8 4 4 **J**
Player B   8 8 4 4 **6**

Both players hold the same 2 Pair – 8s and 4s – but Player A holds a jack kicker, whereas Player B holds only a 6 kicker. Therefore, Player A wins the hand with the higher kicker.

Sometimes, there is more than one kicker involved.

Player A   A A Q **6** 4
Player B   A A Q **5** 2

This time, both players hold a Pair of aces and both hold a queen kicker. But, a poker hand is made up of five cards so, now, attention moves to the next kicker. Again, Player A wins the hand, courtesy of holding a 6 as his second kicker, opposed to Player B's 5. This result is incredibly close. Player A will be blowing the tips of his fingers over this deal; Player B will be licking his wounds.

Perfect Ties

If two or more hands are a perfect tie, the pot is split between all the players involved. This happens more often at Texas Hold 'Em than at many variations because there are five community cards. Let's see an example:

The board shows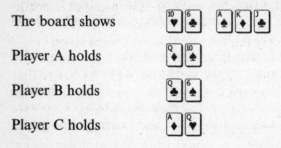

Player A holds

Player B holds

Player C holds

Player A flopped (made the hand when the flop appeared) a Straight (AKQJ10) but, presumably, did not bet enough to keep the other players out of the hand. Unfortunately for him, although the turn did not hurt him, the river certainly did because, now, all three players have the same Straight. Player A may have both Q and 10, but that makes no difference now that the 10 has appeared on the river. All three players can now use the AKJ from the flop and the 10 from the river, to add to their own Q in hand, to make the Straight. The proceeds of this pot will be shared equally between all three players.

Side Pots
Sometimes, when one player has put all his chips into the pot and other players keep on betting, you need to form a side (or secondary) pot. This is how it works.

Let's say that Player X has only $20 left in front of him. Ahead of him, an opponent raises to $50 and another player calls him. Player X wants to call as well, but he can't match his opponents' bets. You can never be driven out of a hand because you don't have enough money on the table – you can always push your last money in and contest the pot. Thus, Player X can only play $20. So, he calls, and goes "all-in". The main pot should now consist of Player X's $20, plus $20 from each of the other players' bets – to match Player X's stake. So, the main pot is worth $60 (plus any Blinds there might have been). This is all Player X can play for, because that covers his stake.

Now, there is a side pot formed from the remaining extra money which the other two players have bet. $30 from their $50 bets goes in there. Obviously, Player X can do no more betting, so he just waits patiently to see the result of the hand. Meanwhile, any further bets made by other players go into the side pot (which may well become far bigger than the main pot). Eventually, the result of the side pot will be decided first and then Player X will show his cards to claim the main pot (or throw them away disgustedly and skulk from the table).

The good news is that online, and in clubs and casinos where there is a dealer, you don't have to worry about these mechanics. It will all be done for you. Although it sounds quite complicated now, they are in fact very simple and you'll get used to them very quickly.

Betting

When you make a bet at poker, it is important to make a verbal announcement as to your intentions. You must state your action clearly and then follow it. This is to stop players fumbling with their chips and watching for a reaction from the other players. You can play with your chips, count them out, flip them in the air but, once you have moved some chips onto the surface of the table away from your own pile, they are deemed to have been bet. You may not take them away again, nor add any more to the pile. For this reason, if you say, "Raise", you can still take your time to decide exactly how much you want to bet. Because you have announced a raise, your bet will be accepted.

Showdowns

When all five community cards have been dealt and there are still two or more players in the hand then, unless one player makes a bet which no one else calls (in which case he wins without having to show his cards), there will be some kind of showdown.

If one player makes a bet and the other player calls, then the *caller* has paid to see the first player's cards. The first player must turn over both his cards for everyone to see. If he has the best hand, the second player usually just throws away his cards and the first player collects the chips.

If, alternatively, the second player has the better hand, he then shows both his cards to everyone and gathers up the pot.

On some occasions, the remaining players all check (no one makes a bet). In this situation, all players should turn over their hands simultaneously. The winner (or winners) is established, and he takes down the money, as we say in poker to mean gathering in the chips from a winning pot.

Sometimes, in this situation, a player hangs back to see who has what. If he then waits until another player thinks he has won the pot and belatedly turns over his hand and claims he is the winner, this is known as *slow-rolling* his hand. It is bad form to do this. If you have won, or think you have won, turn over your cards quickly and claim.

Before we move on to techniques involved in playing Texas Hold 'Em successfully, let's look at the options you have in terms of types and styles of game.

Forms of Game
There are three main forms of poker game:

1. Home Games

As the name suggests, played at home, usually amongst friends, acquaintances and work colleagues. Stakes are usually low and, commonly, the style of poker played changes regularly. One round of Texas Hold 'Em might be played, followed by a Hi/Lo game, then perhaps a mad variation with wild cards. A favourite form is "Dealer's Choice" – where the dealer decides on a different form to be played on each deal.

However, recently, players have come to realize that Texas Hold 'Em is the most exciting form of the game and many home games have switched to playing this form exclusively.

2. Online

At the end of the 1990s very little poker was played online. Now, more poker is being played online around the world than in homes and casinos. It is a massive business, hugely popular, and growing month by month. The advantages are many: there is privacy, convenience (you can play two hands and then change your mind and leave the table again), anonymity, huge choice of games and stakes.

The disadvantages are there too, however: you lose the human, social element, which diminishes many of the psychological elements, such as reading other players' body language and reactions. It is also possible, without the support of others, to lose too much and to become utterly addicted to the adrenalin rush of gambling for high stakes. Like or loathe it, online poker is here to stay.

You can qualify for the World Series of Poker (WSOP) – the World Championships for poker – over the Internet, starting with an entry fee of just $2 and you can give up work and become an online poker pro – as some have – earning a good living from the comfort of your own home.

3. Clubs and Casinos

Beware, the standard of play at poker clubs and casinos will be a lot higher than in your home game or online. You get the atmosphere, the equipment, often a dealer, and the reassurance of high security when you play. You are very unlikely to get cheated in a reputable casino or poker club. However, you'll pay an hourly fee, or the house will take a rake (a small percentage) from each pot, to pay for all the facilities. Playing for mid or high stakes, that's fine, but those fees eat into your bankroll as a low-stakes player and may harm your bottom line. Frankly, steer clear of club and casino poker until you are experienced and competent, or you may lose your shirt.

The Buy-In

Whatever game you play, there is always the buy-in. You exchange cash for chips and you place them on the table in front of you. Traditionally, you do not take chips off the table and put them in your pocket: any that you win are available to be lost until you stand up and *cash-in* (change your chips back into cash).

There is usually a minimum, and sometimes a maximum, buy-in. In clubs and casinos and online, this is posted at the table. In a home game, it will be by mutual arrangement.

Buy-in for an amount which will hurt just a little if you lose and which will please you mightily if you manage to double. Do not buy-in for money you cannot afford. Sometimes the poker gods are in a black mood and you could play perfect poker and lose the lot.

Betting Limits
There are three main styles of betting at poker:

1. Limit Poker
This style is played mainly in poker clubs and casinos in the US. Each round of betting is limited to an exact amount and the number of raises and re-raises is limited also. For example, if the limits were posted as $10/20, that would mean that the Blinds would be $5 and $10 and pre-flop you could only raise $10. When the flop appears, again, only bets of $10 and raises of $10 would be permitted. Following the turn and the river, these bets and raises would then be set at $20. You are not permitted to depart from this structure.

2. Pot Limit
This used to be the form most popular in European card rooms. The Blinds would be set and then the maximum bet possible would be the current value of the pot. If the Blinds were, say, $2 and $5, the first raise you could make would be $7. A subsequent re-raiser would then be able to bet $14 – the total in the pot so far. This meant that initial raises were quite small, but subsequent bets and raises could get very large. This allowed more players to stay in early on and see the flop, but allowed strong hands to drive out weaker players with big bets after the flop.

3. No-Limit

Simply the best. Now, most people play No-Limit Poker in one form or another. This style allows you to bet whatever you like, at any time. If the Blinds are set at $2 and $5, you can push all your money into the middle on a whim. It allows you to exert maximum pressure on your opponents and can lead to huge swings and unbelievably tense decisions.

From the off, playing no-limit, one fact must remain at the forefront of your mind – this could be your last hand, you could be wiped out completely. Every hand you enter must be done wisely, and with courage.

However, the guiding principle is that you can bet only the money that is on the table in front of you. You cannot reach down and suddenly produce more cash from a secret hideyhole. Equally, as with all forms of the game, you cannot be pushed out of a hand, just because you run out of money. Once you have all your money in a pot – you are *all-in* – you compete for that pot up to and including all the betting made until you went all-in. If other players continue to bet, they form a *side pot* of extra bets for which you are not competing. You remain, however, in the main pot and get to show your cards if you have won.

Perhaps the best form of the game is No-Limit with a take-down option. This is proving popular in home games because it combines the excitement of No-Limit with a few prudent safeguards.

You buy-in for an agreed amount – let's say $200 – and, if you win, you are then permitted to remove extra funds over and above that $200. If you are winning, you must keep at least your original stake in front of you to give the other players a chance to win it back. Of course, you can choose to sit out a few hands, or cash-in if you don't want to play any more.

This is the style I recommend as it best combines all the great elements of Texas Hold 'Em Poker.

Tournaments

These are a great way to enjoy plenty of action for a very low risk. If you get lucky and play well, you might win a big prize. Played in clubs, casinos, online and even, sometimes, in home games, a tournament can have four entrants or ten thousand.

Each player pays a small entry fee – say $10 (although some online events are free to enter) – and gets, say, 1,000 chips. Everyone plays, in whatever betting style the tournament may be, until there is only one player left. Traditionally, the winner usually receives between one quarter and one third of the total entry fees, with lower places being paid out on a descending scale.

Online, there are tournaments every minute of the day and night. In clubs and casinos, there are often several scheduled each day. Depending upon the number of entrants, a tournament may take an hour or a week to complete. For more information and some tactics, see Chapter 4.

Now, we've looked at the styles and forms of the game, the betting limits, mechanics, some of the etiquette and terminology, the relative values of hands, and a few rules. It's time to get technical and learn about when to get involved in the action and when to sit back and observe the battle from afar.

3

BASIC STRATEGY FOR CASH GAMES

Your basic strategy is a set of rules to get you off to a good start. As you play and experiment, you will find yourself irresistibly drawn into breaking these rules – and that is fine. As you gain experience and start to develop your own poker-playing personality, you can decide how aggressive or passive you want your style to be. The suggestions contained within this section are designed to get you off to a conservative, sensible start and ensure that, when you play a hand, you are in a strong position from the beginning.

Patience, Patience, Patience
Possibly the single most important skill for a cash game player to learn is patience. I'll say that word again: Patience. There it is . . . a mantra to be repeated through-out your poker playing lifetime. Patience. I'm saying it as much for myself as for you, because, without it, you will live fast and die young – and die penniless. Take a deep breath and say it aloud: Patience.

Some perceive poker to be all about action, all the time. Certainly, there are more heart-stopping, adrenalin-pumping, heart-in-mouth moments in poker than in any other game but they are, for each individual player, relatively rare. Most of the time, you are folding your cards, either before the flop, or once you have seen the flop. You can go hours, even days or weeks, without picking up a decent hand or finding that the flop fits your cards. The expert realizes that this is just the unpredictable run of the cards where normal trends can sometimes seem exceptional. The fact is that every time you sit down to play poker from now on, it's just another few hands in a lifetime of poker. Over that lifetime, you are very likely to pick up close on average hands. So, it is how you handle the bad times, as well as the good, that will determine how successful you are in the long run. Many players can't cope with this and a short run of bad cards sees them starting to play hands that should be discarded, call bets that should be folded, and raise hands as a bluff, just to see some action. This will lose them much money in the long term.

On "Tilt"
Similar is the player on "tilt" – a term flashed up on a slot machine if you attempt, physically, to attack it. This player has lost a few hands in a row, perceived them, rightly or wrongly, to be bad beats (results which seem to defy normal expectation) and starts throwing his money around like a petulant child. Don't think you won't do it, because you will. It happens to all of us sometimes. However, the key is, when it happens to you, to remember the feeling of utter desperation that comes with it, and use

that feeling for the future as a warning signal to get up from the table (or the computer screen) and go do something else for a while.

Starting Hands

As mentioned earlier, by the nature of Texas Hold 'Em, if you start with the best hand, you have a big advantage over your fellow players. Another factor is that, as an inexperienced player, judging what to do once the flop has appeared is quite difficult. The game can become even more difficult when you reach the turn and the river. So, your basic strategy should emphasize the action you take before the flop, either to win you the hand there and then, or to put you in a really strong position for future rounds.

For those reasons, I am going to suggest that you limit the number of hands with which you get involved in the action to just twenty-one. When you don't see one of those hands, you fold (unless you are the Big Blind, in which case, if no one has raised, you're in the hand anyway). Such a strategy requires a high level of discipline because you won't see these hands often. However, when you do enter the fray, you will be placed strongly. These are your key starting hands:

All 13 Pairs AA KK QQ JJ 1010 99 88 77 66 55 44 33 22
AA is the strongest starting hand you can pick up, since with only two cards available, no one can hold a higher Pair than you. This hand, often known as "Pocket Rockets", is what every player hopes to see every time he turns over his cards.

AA KK QQ AK are the premium Pairs; with these and the "Big Slick", AK, it will be good practice always to come into the action by raising – or even re-raising.

Mid-size and lower Pairs can be dangerous, since if higher cards appear on the flop, you may be outdrawn. There are two key ways of playing low Pairs: some good players like to put in a big raise to win the pot there and then; others believe that it is better merely to call the Big Blind or a small raise and hope that you hit a matching card on the flop, giving you Trips – which is a strong hand and may well clean up from everyone who is still in the pot.

I recommend that, generally, you just call.

AQ AJ suited (*suited means that both cards are of the same suit*)

These two hands are just ace-High Cards, but both offer the chance of top Pair draws, top Straight draws and top Flush draws. If an ace appears on the flop, you will have top Pair with a convincing kicker; if the flop is Q high or J high (the highest card showing is Q or J), then you have top Pair with the top kicker. For that strength and the potential to make really strong hands, these cards are worth playing in a Pot Limit or No-Limit Hold 'Em game.

A10 suited   KQ and KJ suited   QJ suited   J10 suited

These are the five weakest starting hands, but I have included them because, although they are not wonderful right now, they have the potential to become strong hands if the top card pairs or if a Straight or Flush draw develops and then completes.

These hands are quite flop-sensitive. If the three cards on the flop don't fit well, you will probably have to abandon your hand the moment there is a bet.

Hands Not to Play
There are so many hands you might get dealt which you certainly should not play. Those containing two different low cards are obviously weak – unless the flop hits them perfectly. It is the mid-range hands that lure players into indiscretions and every mistake you make will likely cost you money. Here are two examples of hands you should not play in any position:

Ace with a low kicker, such as A3 or A6
If the flop comes with an ace and a bet is made by an opponent, or if you make a bet and it is called – you won't know whether you are winning or not. You could easily be outkickered. Almost certainly, you will have to fold, and now you have lost money, and you will be wondering whether you should have folded your Pair of aces.

Picture (or Honour) card with low card, such as K3 or Q6 or J7
Again, you may hit top Pair and then not know whether an opponent has you out-kickered.

The problem with these hands is that they rarely win you big pots but they can lead you into losing big money when you are beaten. Since better poker involves better judgment, and that is a quality which, quite understandably, as a beginner you are lacking, you want to avoid those confidence-draining situations.

Suited Connectors
When you have two cards of the same suit, which are touching in value, such as 9♣ 8♣ or 10♦ 9♦, you have a

low-value hand, but with potential to form a strong, winning hand – such as a Straight, a Flush, or even a Straight Flush.

If and when you become a little more experienced, I would recommend calling the Big Blind bet in a late position (close to the dealer – see next section) and seeing the flop. If the flop hits your hand perfectly, then you have a chance to clean up. If the flop doesn't hit you well, just let the hand go and you've wasted comparatively little in your quest to win a big pot.

There are some players who call bets and even quite large raises with these suited connector hands but, once again, judging what to do after the flop is complicated and best left to those with plenty of experience.

Position
Your position at the table can be vital. Pre-flop, you would like to be the dealer since this allows you to see how many players have called, or have raised, before you decide whether to enter the action. It also means that you have fewer players after you who might raise the betting and force you out of the action. If you are the dealer, or one place to the right of the dealer, in these circumstances, you may consider slipping into the action with weaker hands. These will be shown in the section on Tournaments where your style tends to be freer and more aggressive.

In simple terms, the earlier you are to bet, the stronger you need to be since there is always the possibility that you will be raised and that there will be some callers or even re-raisers. If you make a bet and then, because of raises, you fold your cards (and this will happen reasonably often), you have wasted your initial bet. For that reason, unless you have one of the premium Pairs (AA, KK or QQ) or the "Big Slick" AK – on which you should always raise – in early position, you will be keener simply to call the Big Blind bet and then, if raised subsequently, to call that raise and see the flop.

In mid-position (about halfway between the Big Blind bettor and the dealer) you would loosen up a little bit and, in late-position (the dealer or one seat from the dealer) you might well decide to raise on any of the key 21 hands in an attempt to drive out the Blind bettors and win the pot there and then.

As an example, with a good, but not brilliant hand such as AQ, you might think like this:

You would be unwilling to raise an early position, since there could be stronger hands yet to show themselves and you might well be re-raised. However, if you are on the button (the dealer), or close to him, you might well choose to raise, in the hope of scaring off the Blind bettors and pushing out anyone else who has called on sub-premium hands.

On the Button
If you are the dealer, you are said to be "on the button". This is the most powerful position pre-flop since, other than the Blind bettors (who have been forced to bet), you are the last to act.

A common, aggressive play, when sitting in this position, is to make what is called a "Button Raise".

If there have been no callers from early positions (such calls would suggest better than average hands) and only one caller up to you, it may be worth putting in a button raise to try to drive out the two Blind bettors – who may have terrible cards – and also the caller and steal the pot there and then. Because this tactic often succeeds, players

make these raises on all sorts of sub-standard hands. At
the very least, you should put in a button raise with any of
your 21 starting hands.

Because the tactic is well-known, however, when you
see someone making a button raise, you should be suspicious that he may be trying to steal. Of course, you don't
know if he is bluffing or has a seriously good hand – the
great advantage of raising is that it injects doubt into the
other players' minds. The result of this situation is that
you sometimes get a "double bluff" situation where the
Big Blind re-raises the button raiser even without a particularly good hand. If the button raiser was bluffing –
which is quite often – he probably has to concede at this
stage. And so the constant psychological battle begins
and, at the poker table, it never ends.

Should you get involved in bluffs and counter-bluffs?
Not now. Learn the game: this is only the beginning of a
lifetime's journey. Stick to the low-stake games and you
won't find too many players trying to tie you in knots;
they are all still learning the game themselves.

Calling or Raising?
If you had a choice, you should always prefer to be
raising. There are so many advantages to raising: you may
win the pot there and then; you may drive out threatening
or even better hands than your own. You may be able to
bluff successfully even if the flop misses your hand completely. It sets you on the high-ground – from below,
players will find it hard to attack you.

With the premium hands: AA KK QQ and AK, you
should always raise, even if a player has raised before you.
There are many players who prefer to slow-play strong
hands. This means that they pretend that they have nothing until the end and then attack aggressively, hoping to

lure in weaker hands. Such play is highly risky, very stressful, and extremely hard to judge well. Whilst it does, without doubt, produce some fabulous results sometimes, it also produces disasters in which players can lose a fortune.

Generally, with strong hands like those above, you should protect them by raising and driving out players with more speculative hands which might suddenly overtake you once there are three, four or five community cards with which to work. If no one calls, then the chances are that you would not have made much from the pot anyway. If you get callers, you may be set for some real action – with the odds on your side.

In the final analysis, you will decide what style of poker player you are. You may find that the other players at your table are very respectful of raises and, when you do raise, they mostly fold and concede the pot to you. If that is the case, you might even try raising modestly with all of the 21 chosen hands and seeing what effect that might have on your table . . . Of course, you may discover that you are surrounded by chancers, players who will pay right up to the end to see your cards. These punters are sometimes called "fish" or "fishes": they swim around "fishing" for the perfect card to make their hand a winner. Fish are usually slimy characters, poor, near-penniless souls who have failed to realize that, most of the time at the poker table, discretion really is the better part of valour – and that it is certainly cheaper in the long run.

So, how you act will have as much to do with the style of the other players at your table as the cards you hold in your hand.

How Much to Raise?

You need to be clear in your own mind what you want to achieve by any particular bet. You might want merely to stay in the hand to look at the flop or the turn or river; you may want to build the pot, because you think you have the best hand or are likely to have the best hand at the end. You may want to make a bet to test the reaction of an opponent to try to gauge what he has in his hand; you may want to frighten players out of the action and win the pot there and then.

If you do want to win the pot there and then, the ultimate pressure bet is to go all-in (bet all the chips in front of you). You are unlikely to be called and will win whatever is in the pot already 95 per cent of the time. However, you may get called by a very strong hand, and then you may lose all your money. Generally however, the more you raise, the more you are trying to win immediately. If you raise modestly, you are more likely trying to build the pot because you have the best hand at that moment, or think you will in due course.

A modest pre-flop raise would be two or three times the Big Blind. A medium size raise would be four or five times the Big Blind. A seriously big raise would be more than that.

Post-flop, to bet half the value of the pot, or the whole value of the pot are both standard moves with what you believe to be the best hand at that moment.

Important Note: when I say, "if you feel you have the best hand" that will be a judgment that you, and only you, can make. You will base your decision on a number of factors: you may definitely hold the nuts at this moment; you may have top Pair with top kicker – or 2 Pair, or Trips with a Pair in the hole – and realize that it is very unlikely anyone has you beaten; you may just sense from the other players' demeanour that they have nothing and that your hand is probably winning; you may decide to run a complete bluff because you think no one has anything. You may be wrong. To begin with, you'll be wrong quite often. But, you must form a judgment and then act accordingly. Only poker experience hones this judgment and, having accrued enough experience, then good reading and good practice will turn you from a beginner to an average player and then on, possibly, to the poker heights.

In terms of gauging your raise, simply, the higher you bet, the keener you are to win the pot there and then and not risk being overtaken by opponents when the community cards appear.

Action on the Flop

The time to get off (or out of) a hand is either before the flop – and therefore before you have committed any, or much, money to the pot – or once the flop has appeared and it does not help your hand (which is, I'm sorry to say, most of the time).

The flop is the time when your hand – and those of your opponents – is made or broken. It is the moment when hands which were trailing before the flop have suddenly become strongest, and good hands pre-flop get no help from the community cards and suddenly look frail. Let's look at a series of common situations and decide what action we might take. Bear in mind at all times that different players will take different action in the same situations. There is rarely a right or wrong way to play your hand, just methods that are more or less likely to work. These suggested methods are simple, but they are a good starting place on which to build your own skills and poker identity.

When the Flop Doesn't Hit: Sadly, this is a common situation.

You hold   A♥ Q♣

and the flop comes

If no one bets anything, you can just check and wait to see if the turn and river are great cards for you. An ace would be nice. However, be aware that someone might be holding two spades and be on a Flush draw (hoping that another spade will appear in the turn or river and make him a Flush). If anyone makes a bet, you will have to concede.

You hold

and you raised before the flop, and one player called your raise

and the flop comes

This is a disaster for you. It is very likely that one of the two overcards (cards higher than those in your hand) has paired up with your opponent's hand. If your opponent makes a bet, it will be right to fold and concede your greatly devalued hand. Contrast that with this situation where, again,

you hold

and the flop comes

Now, unless your opponent has AA, KK or a Pair matched on the flop, you have the best hand. You should definitely bet and probably re-raise any bet that your opponent makes since your QQ is likely to be winning. What you do not want to see is a king or ace appear on the turn or river – that would threaten your hand. Here, you want to raise big, to protect your hand and try to force your opponent to fold.

Intention: try to win the pot now with a raise to protect your hand against being beaten subsequently if an ace or king hits the board on the turn or river.

Holding Top Pair: This means if the flop's highest card matches your hand to make a Pair. Now, your Pair is the highest possible unless another player holds a higher Pair in hand (here, only AA in the hole can beat you). This is a common situation which requires a simple course of action. Assuming that there have been no pre-flop raises, but three callers,

you hold　　　　　　K♦ J♦

and the flop comes　　K♣ 9♣ 4♥

when it is your turn you should bet. This is because you hold the top Pair of kings and a decent kicker in the form of your jack. Unless someone has called originally on a strange low hand, or something like K9 or K4, you have the best hand. You do not want to see any further cards in case a third club appears and you begin to fear the Flush. Betting the value of the pot here looks good. If you are called by a player with two clubs in his hand, seeking a club Flush, you have the odds on your side. He will only make his Flush one time in three (see the statistics, on page 92) whilst you have the best hand unless a club appears.

Intention: try to win the pot now or make players pay too dearly to draw to their hand.

Holding an Overpair

An overpair is a Pair in your hidden two cards (in the hole) which is higher than the highest card showing on the flop. Assuming that no one raised pre-flop and you decided to call rather than raise with your low Pair, you face a similar problem to holding top Pair when this happens:

You hold   8♠ 8♦

and the flop comes   7♦ 6♥ 3♦

Hoping that no one has called on 54 or 98 (it has been known) and therefore made a Straight on the flop, you probably have the best hand. Players with a higher Pair than yours might well have raised pre-flop. So, you want to protect your top Pair of 8s from the appearance of high cards on the turn and river, which might mean that another player suddenly overtakes you.

Some players would go all-in here to prevent any speculative calls, but in truth, a large bet – maybe twice the pot size – should do the trick.

Here, your intention is to win the hand now while you seem to be safely in the lead. If you checked or made a small bet which was called and the turn came:

Now you would be miserable. A player might easily hold a king and have you beaten and someone might just have made a diamond Flush.

Anyone betting now will surely have you beat and you will have to give up.

Intention: bet big to win the pot now – you do not want to risk overcards appearing on the table.

Holding Second Pair: Second Pair means that the second highest card on the flop matches with one in your hand to make a Pair. Now, only a player with top Pair, or an overpair, is likely to be beating you. Top Pair is always reassuring but, quite often, no one hits anything much on the flop and the second highest Pair is winning the hand. There are also chances to turn your hand into 2 Pair or Trips. Betting with second Pair can be dangerous, but it can also reap rewards.

You hold   A♠ J♠

and the flop comes   K♣ J♦ 2♠

You might choose to check if you are in early position but, later on, a bet would be in order. If no player holds a king, you may win the pot immediately. If a player holds a king with a low kicker, say K♦ 7♣ (*you* would not be in the hand with that holding of course – unless *you* were the Big Blind), you may frighten him off, making him believe that you also hold a king and probably with a higher kicker.

If you do get called, you have several ways to improve your hand. An ace would give top 2 Pair, another jack would make you Trips, and another spade would give you the Nut Spade Flush draw (if a spade comes on the river you would then have the best possible Flush).

If an opponent raises your bet, you might well choose to lay down your hand. He is likely to hold a king with a good kicker and that means you will be betting against the odds.

Intention: a pre-emptive strike to push out intermediate hands, with some possible draws to improve your hand to a definite winner.

When the Flop Pairs: The flop pairing – that is to say when a Pair appears on the flop – brings tears to even the most robust players' eyes, since any player matching the flop's paired card suddenly holds Trips and is likely to win the pot easily. A paired board (or flop) can also lead to Full Houses overtaking Flushes and casts doubt on all your usual thoughts.

The standard way of betting on a paired board would be as follows:

- If you match the Pair on the board and have made Trips, or better still a Full House, you have made a hand which is very unlikely to be beaten whatever appears on the turn or river. With such a strong hand, it is safe to check to allow other players to stay in the hand, hopefully improve and then feel that it is worth betting or calling your bet later, hence increasing your chances of winning more from the other players.

You hold

and the flop comes

You hope that an opponent might also have a jack in his hand – giving him Trips – or that an opponent has two spades in his hand and subsequently makes a spade Flush. You will beat either of those hands, and you want to give your opponents a chance to make them. Then, when you bet (or they bet) you will get more action and therefore more money out of them.

Intention: lie in wait with the best hand and hope that other players bet or call your bets later.

● If you match the odd card, so making 2 Pair, it is usually right to bet at this stage, because you have 2 Pair when your opponents do not. You do not want them to see the turn or river in case those cards are higher and match with their hands.

You hold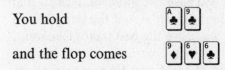

and the flop comes

You now hold 2 Pair but, if you check and allow the turn and river to be dealt, you may see a card higher than the 9 appear.

Intention: win the pot there and then, or make your opponents pay to see cards against the odds.

If, when you make this play, you are raised, you will have to judge whether your opponent holds Trip 6s, or whether he too holds a 9 in hand. If he does, you have the best possible kicker to go with it. Finally, of course, it is possible that he holds a higher Pair in the hole, maybe two 10s or two jacks. If you believe this to be so, you should fold.

A paired board is a fearful situation to the inexperienced. However, this in itself can be an advantage to you. In poker, fear is vital: you can read it in your opponents' faces and in their play. To succeed, you must be fearless. I have made a good deal of money betting paired boards strongly. Imagine you are close to the button.

You hold

and the flop comes

everyone checks around to you so you bet the value of the pot.

You are suggesting that you hold a 4 in your hand and that you now hold 2 Pair. Often, everyone folds and you win. If you get called, beware. The caller is likely to hold an overpair (higher than the 4) or a 9 in his hand. If you get called, you can give up on subsequent rounds.

Your security is that you have two *overcards* – cards that are higher than those on the board – so if the turn shows a 10 or an ace, you may well have the best hand. Generally, to bet in this situation with overcards is sound, but not when there are possible Straight and Flush draws which could destroy your hand, even if you improve, later on.

Many top players might try this action in any position around the table.

Intention: to bluff your way into picking up the pot.

Lower Pairs

I have a simple rule when calling with low Pairs. If the flop produces two or more overcards (cards which are higher than my paired cards), I don't commit any more money to the pot. If there is only one overcard, I may continue pursuing it and if, by some good fortune, all the flop cards are lower than my paired cards, that will be the time to go in with a big raise and try to win the hand there and then, before threatening overcards hit the flop which may beat my hand.

You hold

and the flop comes

It is just too likely someone holds a Pair of queens or 9s. Fold if there is a raise.

Raising to Save Money (or as a Semi-Bluff)
More aggressive players do not always wait until they
have the best hand to put in a raise, they sometimes raise
earlier in the hand, either to push out their opponents
there and then, or to buy themselves some extra time and,
in the long run, save some money. Let's look at an
example:

You hold   A♠ J♠

and the flop comes   Q♥ 6♠ 3♠

Since, at present, you have no hand, you might think that
you would just check and try to see the next card for free
(and sometimes that might be right). However, some
players would reason that, if another spade hits the
board, they have made the top Flush and they put in a big
raise to make their opponents guess whether they have the
best hand now or whether they are on a draw.

The advantage of the raise here is two-fold. Firstly,
everyone may fold, thinking that you have a very strong
hand. This being so, your semi-bluff (you have nothing
now, but the turn or river could bring you a monster)
takes down the pot and you don't even need to see the
next cards to find out if you really were winning. The
second advantage is that, if you get a caller or callers,
they are unlikely to make a bet after the turn card since
they will fear that you will raise them again. So, often
they just check to the raiser (check around to you waiting
to see what you will do) and you then check yourself and
get to see the river card without having had to pay any
more money. In other words, your earlier investment has
had the effect of paying for two cards rather than
possibly having to pay to see both the turn and then pay
again, by calling bets, to see the river.

Even if you do get to see the river and still a spade has not appeared and given you the Flush, because you raised on the flop your opponents may believe that you genuinely do still have the best hand and it may be that one more decent-sized bet from you at the end may be enough to get them to lay down their cards and concede the hand to you on a complete bluff.

All in all, you can see that to check looks safe and conservative but to raise has so many psychological advantages. It's up to you how you want to play – and you certainly do not need to make the same play every time.

Intention: try to win the pot now or make players pay too dearly to draw to their hand.

Holding the Nuts

If you think you have the best hand and you want to make sure that you either win the pot and get paid right now, or, at least, pressure your opponents to pay into the pot in a situation where you believe you have the edge, you make a raise. Strangely, when you have the best hand, and you know for certain that it will be the best hand whatever cards appear on the board, then you have a "lock" on the hand, or, in poker parlance, you hold the "nuts". This allows you to play deceptively because you know that you definitely hold the winning hand. If you told everyone that you had the best hand, they would all fold and you would probably win very little money. Now, you do not want to drive players out of the pot. You want them to stay in and, hopefully, hit a hand of their own. If you can feign weakness or indifference then, if they do hit a hand, they will be betting into you, calling your bets and, generally, paying you more money later than you would get steaming in right away. For example:

if you held

and the flop came

you have a Straight Flush and it cannot be beaten by anyone else. Do not put in a raise now. Just check or call any bet that is made. You hope that someone might hold A♦ and then, if they make a Flush, they will have what they think is the best possible Flush. You, however, have them beaten with your Straight Flush – which is an unbelievably strong hand.

If and when your opponent bets, call the bet and look eager to see the turn or river card. Unlike bridge – and many other games – you can "coffee-house" (mislead your opponents with idle gossip), needle them with taunts, even lie about what you are holding. On the final round of betting, you can put in a small raise, or re-raise and hope to get called or raised again. Whatever happens, you are trying to extricate the maximum number of your opponents' chips on this hand, because you KNOW you are winning.

It is possible that, on such a hand, even if you look bored and don't bet until the final round, no one calls a bet. Unless an opponent has a pretty good hand himself, you are unlikely to see much action. The three diamonds on the flop will scare everyone away.

Your one hope is that one or more of your opponents suddenly gets what he thinks is a great hand. Let's see how this might work. To have any chance of this happening, *you must let your opponents see all the community cards for free.* Say, the turn and river appear like this:

you hold

the community cards are

and one opponent holds

and another

Now, the table is in for fireworks. One opponent has made an ace-high Flush which looks pretty good; another has made a Full House, which beats a Flush, and he thinks he has you buttoned up. One opponent makes a bet, another raises him, perhaps you re-raise. Where will it end? Well, as a Full House beats a Flush, but it does not beat a Straight Flush, hopefully, the end will be you gathering up ALL their chips in a big pile in front of you.

Notice that if you had made a bet on the flop, your opponents might have folded (here, either might have bet on as both have potential), and you would have ended up with a pot only a fraction the size of the one you went on to win.

Intention: to keep your opponents in the hand, hoping that they make a decent hand and are prepared to bet, call, even raise you, so that you make the maximum profit from your dead-cert winning hand.

Action on the Turn and River

If you have stayed in the hand this long, it had better be because you think you have the best hand, you know you have the best hand, or you were on a draw for what would definitely be the best hand (i.e. a Nut Straight or Nut Flush draw). You may still be in the hand because there has been no betting on the flop, but those situations are relatively rare.

Remember that the most costly hands in poker are not those hopeless cards that you pick up 75 per cent of the time; they are the quite good hands you see 20 per cent of the time and you over-value, staying in the pot too long, committing too much money to the pot and then finding it hard to throw your cards away and wave your money goodbye. The most dangerous hands are the second-best hands – because you think that they might be best and then they win you nothing and lose you the most. Therefore, unless you are confident that your hand is best, or will be best on a reasonable draw, if there is a bet from an opponent just throw your hand away now.

On the turn, if you have a hand that you think is best, do not let your opponents get to see the river for free – if they hit their card on the river, you may have converted a winning hand into a losing hand and then find it very hard to judge at the end.

For example:

you hold   A♠ Q♣

and the flop comes   A♣ 6♦ 2♣

As you have top Pair with a good kicker, you put in a bet on the flop and you are called by one opponent.

The turn comes   8♦   A♣ 6♦ 2♣

If you believe you still have the best hand, you should put in another bet and make your opponent pay to see the river card. If you check and he checks, the river appears for free and he may make a Flush or 2 Pair without having had to pay for the risk. For example:

He might hold   A♦ J♠

or   K♣ 10♣

and the river comes

With either of the above hands, you have now been beaten by your opponent: with the first hand, he has 2 Pair – aces and jacks; with the second hand, he has the Nut Flush.

If you had raised the value of the pot, your opponent should certainly have thrown away the Flush draw hand (since he has only a 1/6 chance of making his Flush with one card to come) and he might even have conceded with his AJ.

Either way, to let your opponent see free cards when you think you have the best hand is a mistake.

Betting on the River
When a player bets at the end of the hand, he either believes that he has the best hand and he is trying to get you to commit more money to the pot before he cleans up, or he knows he doesn't have the best hand and is trying to drive you out of the pot because if it came to a showdown, he thinks he would lose. Your job is to judge which he is doing. The answer is not always easy to fathom out, and it will be experience of the game, knowledge of what type of player your opponent is, and the betting so far on the hand, which will guide you to make the best decision.

For now, suffice to say that most inexperienced or intermediate players bet when they have a hand, and usually don't bluff when they don't. So, if your opponent bets, or raises your bet, he believes he has the best hand.

Very good players may bluff at any time and they choose their moments well so that you are never certain what is going on. They may decide to check at the end and then, when you try to make a small bet, they come in and raise you (a check-raise). Now, you don't know whether they are bluffing or trapping you. That play is introduced in the next section.

Generally, if your opponent thinks that he holds the best hand at the end, he bets it.

Check-Raise

A check-raise is usually a very strong move but, like all moves at poker, it can be a complete bluff. With a hand you believe to be best, if you are first to act, you may decide to check, hoping to induce another player to bet (either because he has the second best hand, or on a bluff) and then raise that bet. That will make him think: are you really good or are you bluffing him? Advanced uses of check-raises are tough and not for this book.

Behaviour and Emotions

Keep control of your emotions. Poker can be a huge ego-boosting, adrenalin rush, but it can also be a terrible, confidence-sapping downer. You will, inevitably, experience the extremes of both emotional states, sometimes within a few minutes and a few hands of each other.

If you get hit and lose a big pot, try not to let your opponents see how devastated you are. While you are recovering, do not become morose and depressed – or worse still, angry – but instead ask yourself what, if anything, you did wrong. Could you have played the hand better, or did your opponent just get lucky? If you made a mistake, learn from it; if you played correctly and "took a bad beat", at least take comfort from the fact that you played the hand well and that you are improving your game. Remember that in the short term, there is a lot of luck in Texas Hold 'Em. In the long run, however, the cream will always rise to the top.

If you get beaten, try muttering, "nice hand" or even "very nice hand" – it's a fairly non-committal comment, and it acknowledges the cards, rather than your opponent, so it always has a slight edge to it.

If you win a big pot, particularly if it's a lucky win, don't brag too much. You really don't want everyone staring you down and seeking revenge. Keep your head down and mutter how lucky you are . . .

As for the behaviour of others, poker can be a rough, tough game, though, unlike in the movies, you will probably not see the guns come out at the end of a big hand. You will, however, at some stage face angry, frustrated, losing opponents who claim that you are ignorant, lucky, foolish, incompetent and that you don't know the game. "How could you call?" they'll ask you. If you're good with your tongue, knock 'em dead. If not, smile and tell them you're learning the game . . . Then, resolve to get them again, just as soon as you can.

Above all, don't forget, this is not a genteel parlour game. It's war – hand-to-hand combat – and the pressure never lets up. If you don't like the sound of that, it's time to look for a different kind of game.

RECOMMENDED STARTING HANDS FOR CASH GAMES

Here is the very basic guide to starting hands and the action you might take with them. As you gain experience, you will modify these actions to take into account your opponents and what you have learnt about them.

Premium Starting Hands
AA KK QQ AK
Always RAISE in any position; always RE-RAISE in any position.

Good Starting Hands
JJ 1010 AQ suited
CALL in early positions; RAISE in late position; CALL small raises; consider RE-RAISING a button raise or a late-position raise.

Other Starting Hands
99 88 77 66 55 44 33 22 AQ AJ suited
CALL in most positions; consider a RAISE in late position and on the button. CALL (and consider RE-RAISING) small raises and button raises.

Weakest Starting Hands
KJ suited   QJ suited   J10 suited   KQ suited
CALL in all positions, FOLD if raised by a player in early position.
FOLD if the flop does not hit encouragingly (2 Pair, Straight or Flush draw), and there is a raise.

4

TOURNAMENTS

How a Tournament Works

Tournament poker has gone from being the preserve of the elite a few years back, to being a favourite form of the game for the masses.

In 1949, the legendary gambler, Nick Dandalos – more famously known as Nick the Greek – ambled into Vegas looking for a truly enormous game of poker. He approached Benny Binion, who owned the infamous Binion's Horseshoe Casino, and Binion decided that he would set up a game for Nick the Greek on one condition: it was played in public so that everyone could watch. Nick the Greek agreed and Binion contacted his old friend, Johnny Moss. Moss was considered the world's greatest player then and he hurried from his game on the other side of the country to play. Binion's idea to have the challenge played in public turned out to be a stroke of genius. Punters flocked into his casino to watch vast sums of money being bet. They, in turn, stayed for a while, played a little Blackjack or dice and made Binion's bottom line swell.

Johnny Moss and Nick the Greek played for about five months, occasionally allowing other players who could afford a minimum buy-in of $10,000 (this is in 1949) to join them. No one knows how much Moss won, but it ran to seven figures. Nick the Greek – evidently a fine gambler – eventually stood and shook Moss's hand and said, "Mr Moss, I have to let you go."

Twenty years later, Binion staged the first World Poker Championship. Johnny Moss won that year and twice more and, to date, he is one of only two players to have won the main event three times.

During the 1970s, a handful of players contested the WSOP – the World Poker Championships. Nowadays, thousands line up in Las Vegas each May – paying the $10,000 entry fee – wondering whether this year will be their year to land the "Big One". Long before that, hundreds of thousands of players have competed in quali-fying events, or *Satellites*, trying to win a seat in the big tournament final itself. The WSOP final now runs for five days and the winner will not only have been skilful and lucky but will also require enormous powers of concen-tration and stamina.

Thankfully, there are many, less stressful tournaments in which to compete and to hone one's skills. The big advantage of tournament play is that you pay one fee and that is usually all you stand to lose. This means that you could enjoy hours of exciting poker action all for a $5 or $10 entry fee. If you happen to win, or even reach the final table, you will be in the money.

Whether you play in a club or casino – or arrange your own home tournament – or even online, the structure will be the same. Each player pays an entry fee and receives 1,000 or 1,500 chips in exchange. Once you lose your chips, you are out. There are, on occasions, tournaments where, if you go bust within the first hour, you can *re-buy* – when you pay the entry fee again and get more chips. Other players like re-buys because they boost the prize pot. Sometimes, after an hour, you can *add-on* to your chips by paying a premium price to top up your total. Many serious players do this, but it is far from compulsory. Usually, however, you get your chips and it's your duty to try to add to them until, ideally, you have everybody else's chips in front of you in one big – either actual or cyberspace – pile.

Unlike cash play where the Blind bets stay the same and you are able to stay in the game for as long as you like, tournament poker ups the action with what are called *Blind Levels*. This simply means that, after a given time (perhaps every ten minutes, perhaps every hour), the Blind bets are increased to higher and higher levels. For example, they might start at 10/20, then move to 20/40, then to 50/100, and then on to 200/400 and so on. This forces players to gamble on sub-standard hands because, if they just sat there, eventually they would spend all their money on the Blind bets and get wiped out. So, the action in a tournament starts slowly (when the Blinds are low) and then builds and builds, becoming increasingly frantic as the Blinds begin to get higher until all but the most successful players are knocked out. Because of this system, two characteristics come to the fore in tournament poker: aggression and luck. Without these two, you will be doomed. The good news is that because luck plays a greater part than usual in any given tournament, even a modest player has a chance to do well. However, take note: the same group of the world's top players regularly make it to the final tables of major events. That, clearly, is far more than luck.

Online, you can play in tournaments 24 hours a day, with low entry fees and with anywhere from six to 6,000 entrants. In poker clubs and casinos, the card-room manager will be able to tell you when their tournaments take place.

Tactics

As with everything in poker, there are many different ways to approach a tournament. In this section we'll take a look at some key factors to have in the back of your mind as you play your first few tournaments. As you develop as a player, so your style of play will be refined and you can decide which style of tactics to employ.

Early in the Tournament

There is much more bluffing in a tournament than in a cash game because you don't have time to wait for the good hands. You have to get in there and start applying pressure. The battle to increase your chips starts from the first hand and never lets up. Take your eye off the ball for a moment and someone else will overtake you or steal your chips.

However, during the first few betting levels, when the Blinds are low, many players like to wait for good starting hands to try to get them off to a winning start. Therefore, you can afford to be aggressive early on as players are less likely to call you when they feel they could fold their hands and wait for a better opportunity to get involved.

Some players use the all-in weapon frequently at this stage. There is a Small Blind, a Big Blind, one caller, and then suddenly they push all their chips into the centre. Who wants to call that? Maybe they have AA – pocket rockets – maybe they are on a complete bluff. Ninety-nine per cent of the time, everyone folds and they make a small profit. This doesn't seem right to me – the risk/reward factor seems out of kilter: to risk all your chips just to earn a few. It only takes one good hand, or one speculative bettor, to wipe you out.

By way of an example, playing online in one tournament, having seen no decent cards whatsoever and sitting in first position, I picked up A♣ Q♣ and decided just to call. Sure enough, on the button, a player, who had gone all-in twice before already, decided to make the play again. I called. When there is only one player who is not all-in – and therefore there can be no more betting – players turn over their cards and the community cards are revealed with everyone watching the action. This heightens the excitement for everyone. To cut the long story short, my opponent had made this play with K♦ 10♦ – frisky to say the least – and the community cards helped neither of us, so I doubled through with an ace-high hand. My opponent had a few chips left (as he had more chips than me before going all-in) but soon got knocked out, and I went on to reach the final table.

So, in short, be aggressive, raise substantially, be prepared to bluff early in the tournament, but don't risk all your chips unless you really have to.

In Mid-Tournament

After the first hour (sometimes two) there will be a short break – even online – to give players a chance to rest for a few minutes, grab food, or head for the rest rooms. If you've made it to the first or second break, you've settled down and established yourself in the tournament now. However, it is essential that you remember that you must keep trying to add to your chips because, with the Blinds rising, you will soon be losing ground.

If you want to work out how you are doing, you can try this simple calculation (online, there will be a page which tells you all of this at the click of a mouse). Take the number of competitors who entered the event and multiply that by the number of chips with which everyone started. Then, assess how many people remain and divide those chips by the remaining players. That will give you the average chip count and tell you whether you are keeping up or not.

For example, at the second break, the tournament organizer announces that there are 70 players left. There were 210 entrants, who each got 1,000 chips. So, the average chips now should be 3,000. If you have more, you're ahead of the game (for now); fewer, and you need to be placing your foot on the accelerator and leaving it there – at least for a while.

By this time, somewhat alarmingly, even to call a basic bet will cost you a large amount of chips, but you must remember that the figures involved will increase continually throughout a tournament and you must adjust accordingly. When you had 1,000 chips, you were prepared to call for 50 (one twentieth of your total) or make a raise of 200. Now that you have, say, 4,000, you must be prepared to call for 200, or make a raise of 800, because that is still the same proportion of your chips. In fact, if anything, you will have to increase the proportion of chips you risk in order to stay in the game. You must be fearless. Those chips are just a way of keeping score. They are not yours and you cannot cash them in for money until you've survived to the end and made it to the final places. Think of them only as tokens which must be won in order to succeed.

As the Blinds rise and players become *short-stacked* (well below the average number of chips at any given stage), they become more and more desperate to enter the action and try to double through. You should focus on these players and attack them to try to knock them out of the tournament. There are two reasons for this: Firstly, they will take more risks because time is running out for them. Secondly, even if they win the pot, because they are short of chips they won't knock you out of the event.

Chip and a Chair

It's a poker expression. If you still have a chip in front of you, then you still have a chair at the table and that means you are still in the tournament. Who knows, you might just double your chips a few dozen times and end up winning. It's been done, and it'll be done again.

My record is losing 948 of my 1,000 chips within the first fifteen minutes of a tournament (leaving me just 52) and going on to beat 39 other players to win. Was I lucky? You bet. Could I do it again? Maybe. Was it satisfying that I never gave up and triumphed in the end? Obviously – that's why I'm telling you about it. The moral: never give up until that last chip has gone.

Short-Stacking

After that thrilling tale of derring-do, we return to reality. If you get short-stacked, you will be attacked by the stronger, richer players and you will be in trouble. One of the key disadvantages you will have is that you will lose the ability to exert pressure by making a big bet or raise. If you only have a few chips, people will call you because they can afford to. If they get lucky, you're out.

The secret is not to let yourself get short-stacked in the first place. Let's say you start with 1,000 chips and nothing good happens to you for the first hour and you are hanging in there. You're down to 400 chips. Don't just sit there and let yourself get so short-stacked you are totally at the mercy of the cards. Get your chips in there and try to double through and get back on even terms. So, avoid short-stacking by aggression. Either you're back in it, or you go out, but that choice is better than just being whittled away.

Pot Odds

This means, what you stand to gain for the price of a bet. Take this example of a hand from an online tournament.

I held Q♣ 10♣ and had 460 of my 1,000 chips left. I was planning to wait for another, better, hand to try to double through, but on this hand there was a raise to 300 and three callers. So now, for the price of 300 chips, I stood to win 1,500. All of a sudden Q10 becomes a playable hand because of what you stand to gain in return for a modest investment. I called and the flop came:

Oh joy! The top Straight; no chance right now of a Flush to beat me, nor a whisper of anything better.

One player raised all-in himself, three players folded and I called for my last 160 (so the hand must be played out). The poor chap had AJ and thought two top Pairs ought to be pretty good. The turn and river made no difference so I quintupled through and was right back in the fray.

Look for the chances to multiply your money three- or four-fold and be prepared to enter those pots with more modest hands.

Towards the End

The Blinds will be huge and the size of the pots dizzyingly high. Remember that you are not betting cash, just tokens. Be fearless and aggressive and continue to abide by the normal principles – just exaggerated and more determined. Everyone will be playing dodgy hands and trying to frighten everyone else. Just roll with it.

Be aware of the payouts for the tournament. You might be in the money if you make it to the last 100 players – or you might have to finish in the top three. It'll all depend on the number of entries and the agreed pay scale. When it gets close to the money, players will be desperate not to be knocked out just short of a payout so, if anything, that's the time to bully them by raising pre-flop and pretending that you are strong. However, do not enter pots when players with lots of chips are competing; they'll be there because they have good hands and are hoping to improve their position. Players who are short-stacked are in pots, just trying to survive – they are the players to attack.

If you are short-stacked, and only one or two places away from getting into the money, you might well decide to tighten up, hope that other players get unlucky and knocked out before you, and you creep into the money.

All players can tell you such stories, but my biggest tournament disappointment was online. I was in a satellite event qualifying for a seat in the WSOP, together with ten nights in a five-star hotel in Las Vegas – a package worth about $13,000 – not the biggest prize for which I have ever had a genuine shot, but a pretty cool one. There were 790 entrants and eight seats to be won. The ninth place player won about $4,000 in cash. You guessed it. I made it to the final table (of ten players) and got knocked out first – in tenth place! Twelve hours of play (I'd qualified for that satellite through another one costing just $20) and I emerged with nothing. I felt nauseous and my little dog didn't look me in the eye for the next two days . . .

Sometimes it just goes that way, but be aware of where you are and how you are doing at all times.

Chip Counts and Other Pressure Plays

In live events, an opponent may ask you for a chip count before he decides what to do. Good players will assess how much you have, how much they have, how much they stand to win, and what will happen if they lose. They'll work out the odds of the situation before taking action. If you are asked for a chip count, just add up your chips and tell them – or let the dealer do it. You are required to keep your chips in view at all times anyway so your opponent probably knows the answer to the question already. He's doing it to intimidate you, to watch your reaction, to gauge your body language, maybe just to needle you. From the outset, learn to ignore any comment that is made at the table. Comments are always irrelevant unless you know the guy making it and you can read him like a book. Since that is a very rare situation, learn from the outset: take no notice of comments, coffee housing, barbs, or taunts. Just play your game doing whatever you had planned to do anyway.

The Final Table

All tournament players want to reach their nirvana: the final table. In a major tournament, you'll be guaranteed a big payout if you reach the final ten (sometimes eight). Players at the final table can congratulate themselves on getting so far and they know that, with just a couple of lucky hands at the right moment, they could swoop into the lead. However, at no-limit Hold 'Em, the swings can be huge and you can be in the lead one moment and out of the tournament the next.

The Blinds will be huge – you may even have automatic ante bets (bets which every player must make before each deal to build up the pot still further) so your stacks will be blitzed, constantly under attack. Keep betting strongly and confidently and ignore the sums at stake. When you're betting 25,000 just to call, it's all a bit dizzying, but then you must remember that all the chips from all the other players have ended up on this final table, divided amongst just these last players, so of course the stakes will be high.

Short-Handed Games and Heads Up
The moment that you reach the last four or five players, the game is said to be short-handed. The effect of this is to increase the value of all poker hands, since the likelihood of a really monster hand being dealt is far less. So, you will start to play hands that you would usually throw away.

By the time you reach the last two players, where you are playing head-to-head or *Heads Up*, even a jack in your hand looks good. An ace or king is strong, even with a poor kicker; any Pair is huge. The only way you'll learn to play aggressively enough to win a heads up challenge is by practising. I lost my first eight heads-up finals but, now, I'm in there with a decent chance of winning the lot. You need to raise, raise, raise – constant, unremitting aggression and sharp decision-making. Personally, I prefer real-life heads up, because I can see my opponent, but online it is still exciting to the very end.

So, that's what you'll face if you make it that far. Now, let's take a look at one or two differences between the cash game and a tournament.

Tournament Starting Hands
In a tournament, you should be prepared to call more small bets in order to see the flop, since there is a real hurry to make a decent hand quickly in order to get you off to a good start.

To play just our 21 starting hands from our cash game strategy, as shown on page 65, would be too restrictive.

You might not see one before you ran out of chips. So, to those 21 hands, let's add a few more which offer a chance of bringing in the pot:

Suited Connectors: Two cards of the same suit, touching each other:

You probably shouldn't go much lower than 87, although I did play 5♣ 4♣ once and hit 554 on the flop. However, just because I got lucky once doesn't make it the right play. You'll see the flop co-operate beautifully with lousy hands you've thrown away and you mustn't be phased by it. You were right to throw away a bad hand and, normally, nothing on the flop would change your mind. When it does, just remember the hundreds of other times when it would have lost you money.

Suited almost-Connectors: I'm not sure that this is an official poker term, but it sums up what I mean: two cards of the same suit, almost touching:

Both these hands, and the proper suited connectors, are very flop-sensitive. Unless you hit 2 Pair, or a Straight or Flush draw (or a Straight and Flush on the flop), then you'll probably have to give up. However, when you do hit a hand, it's usually big and you have the potential to cause real damage to your opponents' chip stacks.

Ace and a Small Kicker – Suited: I hate these hands myself, but many good players like getting involved with them. They often raise with these hands in tournaments and then bet them strongly if they hit the flop at all (that is to say, if the cards on the flop improve their hand).

If you gain a Flush or Flush draw or 2 Pair, you're in good shape but, if an ace hits the board, you'll never be quite sure someone doesn't have an ace with a higher kicker (what we might call a "higher ace"). That situation can cost you all your chips.

Ace and a Small Kicker: I wouldn't play these hands except in late position when I was desperate, and then, frankly, I know my nerves will be frayed by the end of the hand.

The good news is that, if you hit an ace, you might have the best hand by far and you might win a decent pot. Some people play that if they hold a Pair of aces between them and the board, it'll be the best hand unless there's been an early raise. Generally, this tactic will work quite well but it is only a matter of time before they are out-kickered (another player has an ace with a higher kicker) and, when that time comes, it may cost them all their chips!

I can't bring myself to recommend any other hands to play, even when desperate in a tournament. However, there are plenty of people who'd make a big raise on any two lousy old cards and then follow it up with another big raise after the flop. Do it with enough confidence and, unless you are unlucky, you'll probably take down the money. But it takes guts and the perfect poker face.

Late Position Calling

Because, to succeed in a tournament, you need to gamble more to hit winning hands, many players become much "looser" (happy to speculate), especially when they are one or two seats to the right of the dealer. Hoping that, with only three or four players left to bet, no one will raise, such loose players call and, more often, raise with what would normally be considered medium-poor hands, such as:

ace and a low kicker A4 A2

king or queen with a high kicker K10 K9 Q9

non-suited connectors

very low suited connectors

If the flop hits perfectly, they can win a very big pot. However, for the vast majority of the time, the flop is totally unsuitable and they have to concede.

   Basically, don't play these hands unless you are under pressure in a tournament or rich and like to play fast and loose . . . or just very lucky.

5

TELLS

A "tell" is a physical signal given, usually unconsciously, at times of stress.

If you knew what cards your opponents were holding, poker would be a far more rewarding game. It might not be as exciting but who cares when you would be rich beyond your wildest dreams. The world's best players seem to know what their opponents are holding, even before the first bets are made. Some of it is bravado designed to put off their opponents, but most of it is sheer skill at the reading of body language. Professional players note every movement, every expression, every heartbeat (sometimes literally; the pulse in your neck can reveal how you feel about your hand and how the deal is developing). This is why so many players wear sunglasses even in darkened, smoke-filled rooms – to hide their eyes.

Incidentally, the WSOP, like many other big poker events, has now become non-smoking. Basically, I'm sure that this is desirable but it does affect the atmosphere of the room, making it seem sterile. In the UK, one TV company has decided that a poker room needs smoke so, for their televised tournament, they are pumping dry ice onto the set to make it look like a smoke-filled dive!

Once you reach the dizzy heights of top-level poker, you will be aware of the many indications which other players give away but you may not yet be cognisant of every message you are, subconsciously, broadcasting. The best players have complete control over their bodies, their breathing, their blinking. This is all a little high-falutin' for our home games and friendly tournaments but, there is no doubt that, if you start observing your opponents and matching what you see to what happens subsequently, you can start building your bank of information that much more quickly. When you get good, that will pay dividends.

How to Behave at the Poker Table
First impressions are important – and no more so than at poker. An image is a particularly important thing at the poker table and not only your own. Having tried many such images for myself over the years I have come to realize, somewhat sadly, that there is one far more success-ful than any other: total confidence: be it loud and brash or quiet and concentrated. Talking a good game, parrying every comment, almost arrogance. I have tried to act small, disinterested, feigning weakness – and then striking like a cobra – but it just doesn't work.

Get comfortable, feel happy with yourself and prepare to enjoy yourself whatever happens. If you get lucky and it's commented upon, agree vigorously: "I am a very lucky player." Many poker players look miserable, convince themselves they are unlucky, believe that their cards are far poorer than everyone else's and, if they could just get their share, they'd clean up. Don't, whatever you do, try to dissuade them from such a notion. The more deluded, depressed and downright miserable your opponents, the more likely they are to hand over their money to you.

"Mad" Mike Caro, billed as "the legendary mad genius of poker", quotes his first rule of poker conduct as: If your opponents "are helpless and they can't defend themselves – you're in the right game!"

This is another reason why I like to raise a lot, especially early on in the game. It hammers home the impression that I'm happy with my lot, my cards and the way the game is going. In fact, the happier I seem, the more confident I appear, the more positive about the whole experience I can be, the more it will disrupt and dismay my opponents.

Key Tells
There are millions of tells. Some are universal, some deeply personal to you or to a particular opponent. Here are some key tells which you may care to bear in mind as you begin to try to form your impression of your opponents:

Opposites Attract
The most basic tell, most commonly practised by less experienced players is to act directly opposite to the way you think you should. When strong, you try to appear weak; when weak, strong.

For example, bluffs often get bet loudly and forcibly and quickly – the chips go in hard and your opponent tries to look tough. Bets or raises holding the nuts take a long time to make and chips are often pushed reluctantly, almost surreptitiously, onto the table. Once you notice this in action, you'll wonder why anyone bothers but, in truth, it's just us, as human beings, trying to be deceptive. Real poker players spend their whole lives being deceptive but, for most of us, with jobs and families and friends, we try to act squarely most of the time. When it comes to lying, subconsciously we think we'd better cover it up. Spot this for the first time and smile (inwardly) at how obvious it is.

The same applies to the revelation of emotion, especially amongst those who usually stay relatively poker-faced: players sitting up and acting interested when the flop hits the table have usually missed their hand; players sighing, mumbling, grumbling and generally looking sad, are usually happy.

Amazingly, this is a tell which can be read even in online poker rooms. You have to be aware of server reaction times and be aware of the usual betting style and patterns of your opponent but, once again, bluffs and fishes nearly always get bet fast; top hands and nuts get bet slowly, the bettor often waiting until virtually the last moment to signal his bet. He's trying to indicate uncertainty – and it almost always means the opposite.

Eyes

Keeping a close eye on your opponents is vital and can be make-or-break when you come to bet. The time you use to decide what action to take is also a time discreetly to observe your opponents. One of the simplest tells is based on the attention being paid to your betting by other players. If a player is looking away, or seems to be looking away, from you while you are betting, this often demonstrates strength. On the other hand, a player who seems to be looking at you closely is often weak. The psychology is relatively simple. A player with a strong hand, which he thinks is winning, really doesn't care much what you bet, since he is going to call or raise anyway based on his cards. A player planning to bluff, or fish for the pot against the odds, is much more concerned about what you do. He may be looking for any sign of weakness in your betting so that he can leap in with a big bluff to drive you out, or limp in to see another card.

Noise and Silence
Noisy tables are often loose. Everyone is having a good time and some players are just there for the sheer fun of it. You, on the other hand, are there to win. I make a beeline for a noisy table. If, however, a vociferous player goes quiet, or even just quieter, more often than not, this signifies a strong hand. Subconsciously, he is rallying his faculties to make the most of a good situation: something he need not do if he is just hanging around the pot fishing, or trying to bluff you out of the pot. When a loud opponent goes quiet, beware.

Conversely, when a usually quiet opponent gets talking, this is likely to cover the fact that he has a weak hand. He wants to appear "normal", relaxed and confident. Look out for statements which are embellished, over-emphasis of words or syllables. The police will tell you that anyone proffering too much information, or going into too much detail, is usually trying to hide other knowledge or to divert attention to another matter. Subconsciously, this is what we tend to do.

Speed, Staring, Mouths and Intimidation
A whole raft of likely bluffs here:

● Players who call very quickly (both online and at the table) usually have something, but not that good a hand. They're trying to tell you that they're good. But, if they were, they wouldn't really want to tell you.

- Players, having made their bet, who stare at their opponent, usually want him to fold. If you wanted a call, you might well let your opponent relax.
- Covering your mouth or nose, inadvertently, is a classic body-language tell of uncertainty and distortion. It's the same at the poker table. However, this tell is often bluffed by those in the know.
- Players who try to direct their intimidation at one other player are usually bluffing. It's a macho thing and the rationale is that it is easier to fold and not lose face than to call and then have to deal with a noisy, gloating opponent.
- A special online tip is one garnered from many hours of observation. Players who make raises or bets with carefully counted out amounts, say $9.99 or $16.34 seem to be bluffing a very high proportion of the time.

Be aware, not only that these are tells that you can use against your opponents, but also that they can be used against you. Don't spend so much time analysing your opponents' behaviour that you spend no time on your own.

"Putting" an Opponent on a Hand

Trying to gauge what cards your opponent is holding is a combination of reading body language, interpreting betting, and looking for clues in the behaviour of your opponent. It takes a lifetime to master and the only proven method is practice, over years and years. Each time you are in a pot and there is a raise pre-flop, decide what you think your opponent might be holding and compare that with his hand if you get to see it. Do this also on those many hands when you are not involved in the action. Don't daydream – watch the action and learn from it.

Every time, post-flop, there is betting and raising and re-raising, observe carefully, using the information on tells above, and build a picture of how players generally, and the specific player involved, act in particular situations. As you do this, your reading of your opponents' hands will improve.

It is important actually to name out loud (in your head) what you think a player holds, otherwise you'll find yourself nodding sagely and thinking, "Well, I knew it was something like that . . ." Something like that isn't good enough, so name those cards and compare what you thought to reality. Keep doing it – all the time.

As a hand progresses, it should become easier to identify the hand your opponent holds. However, the earlier you can do it, the more money you will win, and the more you will save.

I have a confession to make: I find it hard to read my opponents' cards, especially online and in tournaments, where people tend to play quite loosely, call on substandard hands and bluff more frequently. However, poor though I may be, I notice a small improvement each time I devote a solid period of time to serious play. That is what every poker player must aim for.

Bad Beat Stories

What is a "bad beat"? It's when, against the odds, an opponent overtakes you and wins the money that, rightfully, should be yours. Every player suffers bad beats, virtually every session. The fact is that the odds may dictate that five times out of six you'll win, but that sixth time may just appear. Since you are playing these kinds of odds routinely, the unlikely will, on occasion, appear to occur consistently. The important thing to remember is that it happens to everyone and, although you are certain it happens to you more often than anyone else, if you are playing correctly, in the long run, the odds will come true and you will be a winner.

Your friends and opponents will want to share their bad beat stories with you – it's human nature. They are looking for sympathy and my advice is, to your friends, give it to them, enthusiastically, loudly and dogmatically. "It's disgusting how these fishes get lucky; that's appalling; that's so dispiriting, don't let it get you down." My advice is get in with these heartfelt platitudes halfway through their story, because you know what they're going to say and this will cut it short.

To your opponents, I recommend a different strategy. Don't agree with them; don't disagree with them. You want to get them thinking because, if an opponent isn't thinking about the game, then his chips are more likely to move towards your stacks. I'd nod sagely, indicate the offender and go with something like: "He's a canny player, always up to something . . ." This gets both the complainer and the offender thinking . . . or even "Well, yes, but I guess you could have played the hand differently . . ." That might get you into trouble, but it will also cause your opponent to re-think the hand when he probably played it just fine. More importantly however – much more importantly – you are paying the offending opponent a small compliment. Bad beats come about because the player with the worse hand is still in a pot which he should have left earlier. You do not, repeat DO NOT, want to discourage this. You hope he'll carry on staying in pots too long because, sooner or later, the luck will desert him and so will his chips.

I am consistently amazed at the behaviour of players in online poker rooms. Virtually every time I play, I encounter a player at my table who seems hell-bent on giving away his chips. He may be a beginner, a rich fool, or just on tilt after eight hours of misery and no cards. He may be a constant raiser, or a constant caller. I see players who play every single hand they are dealt – without exception. These people are a licence to print money for you. You just have to hang around, play reasonably tight – don't try to bluff weak players, they just don't get it – and wait to get paid. Yet I have seen other, better players, criticising, whining and insulting these goldmines until, frightened and offended, they leave the table. What madness is that? Nurture ignorance, congratulate them, stroke their egos – do anything to keep them there.

Finally, keep your bad beat stories to yourself. Everyone has heard them before, however outrageous the occurrence. More than that, whoever you choose to tell probably had a hundred times more riding on their hand than yours, so just don't!

There is, however, one – slightly skewed – bad beat story I do like, recounted by Anthony Holden in his wonderful book *Big Deal*. Eric Drache, a hugely successful and popular (those two don't often go together) high-rolling poker player recounted a story where, deep in a heavy-duty game in Vegas, his wife called him to tell him that she'd just pranged their brand-new Jaguar. Drache consoled his wife, checked that she was all right and suggested she just wait until the insurance sort it out.

"But . . ." she wailed, "our beautiful Jaguar is ruined."

Drache apparently replied: "Honey, right at this moment, I'm stuck for four beautiful Jaguars – go call the insurance!"

6

PERCENTAGES AND ODDS: UNDERSTANDING YOUR CHANCES

If you want to play poker to be a hero or to live out a glamorous image of the game: smoking guns, wads of $100 bills, shiny sports cars and the like, then you can. You can pour money into pots hoping to get rich and look smart. Occasionally, you will succeed and it will feel wonderful. For the vast majority of the time, however, you will lose and, occasionally, you'll lose badly. Strangely, the wads of those playing against you will grow large and yours small. Strangely – since you are such a hero – you will go broke and the bad guys will get rich. This is because playing poker to win is a long-term, unglamorous pastime which the pros do extraordinarily well and they do it all the time. Playing the odds, playing the percentages and, crucially, playing the people.

Success at poker is as much a matter of avoiding mistakes as it is coming up with inspired brilliancies. Only you will be able to decide whether you can sit tight and be patient enough to improve your game, hone your skills and win in the long term. If you think you can, then some basic percentages are in order. Many top players are aware of every percentage chance at every moment of the game but, for us, just a basic knowledge will help to form us as players.

Since the key moment on any Hold 'Em hand is when the flop appears, let's look at a table of statistics which can help you to decide whether it is worth staying in the pot or whether this is the right time to bow out gracefully and inexpensively.

PERCENTAGE CHANCE OF GETTING THE CARD YOU NEED

Number of Outs	2 cards to come (%)	1 card to come (%)
20	67.5	43.5
19	65	41.3
18	62.4	39.1
17	59.8	37
16	57	34.8
15	54.1	32.6
14	51.2	30.4
13	48.1	28.3
12	45	26.1
11	41.7	23.9
10	38.4	21.7
9	35	19.6
8	31.5	17.4
7	27.8	15.2
6	24.1	13
5	20.4	10.9
4	16.5	8.7
3	12.5	6.5
2	8.4	4.3
1	4.3	2.2

What is an "Out"?

It's a card which will get you "out" of a sticky situation and make your hand the best, the winner. Sometimes called "Out Cards", you will often hear players saying, "That was unlucky, I had 16 outs and I hit none of them . . ."

Using Pot Odds and Drawing Odds

As described earlier, Pot Odds is your basic method of assessing what you stand to gain by continuing in the hand – if you have read the hand correctly – opposed to what it will cost you to continue playing.

For example, let's imagine you hold an ace and another spade and the flop comes K84 with two spades. You now have a Flush draw. If you make it (if the turn or river brings a spade) you will have the hand won. However, before you have a chance to decide what to do, a player in front of you raises the pot. Is it worth playing, or is it worth folding? It all depends upon how much is in the pot and how much more you have to bet to stay in.

Let's say that three players called the Big Blind of $5, making a total of four players in the hand and $22 in the pot ($2 from the Small Blind). Two players check and then your left-hand opponent bets $10. Is it worth calling (or raising) to stay in the pot?

Consult the chart: there are nine spades left in the deck, any of which would almost certainly win you the hand. The chart tells you that with two cards to come and nine "out" cards – cards which will get you out of the hole you're in right now – there is a 35 per cent chance of a spade appearing. That means that to pay $10 to stay in a pot that is already $30 is worth doing. If you make your hand, you may win even more.

On the other hand, if the bettor had pushed $40 into the pot, it really doesn't look worth the bet. Forty dollars to stay in a pot worth $70 dollars – you'd need well over a 50 per cent chance to want to do that usually.

A Flush draw usually has nine cards to complete the hand, offering basic odds of 35 per cent with two cards to come and 19.6 per cent with just one card to follow.

Implied Pot Odds

This takes the theory further and says that not only should you consider how much money is in the pot, but also how much more money may end up there, and it is on that basis that you should judge whether to play on. It's a looser system, but it should still guide you away from silly bets and into better ones. Whereas a Flush draw can sometimes seem very obvious to the other player and this results in you not gaining any extra value from the pot, Straight draws and two low Pairs can often be completed without anyone feeling suspicious and then you have the chance to increase the size of your win if you make your hand. For example:

You hold

and the flop comes

There's only $10 in the pot and an opponent bets $10 now. There are eight cards that can help you (four kings, four 8s). That looks like a 31 per cent chance but, players will ask themselves, surely if I make a king or an 8 on the turn or river, I'll coin it in. Your opponent may well not consider a king – and especially an 8 – a threatening card and you may well generate one if not two or three further bets out of your opponent. In other words, the implication is that the pot isn't really worth $20 when you bet into it, it's potentially worth a lot more. That's why you might well choose to call (or raise as a semi-bluff) in such a situation.

Conversely, you might have the same hand and flop but now your opponent goes all-in for $15. Now, the hand looks much less good. You would have to bet $15 into a $25 pot and you know that you can't get any further money out of your opponent as he is all-in. That's 60 per cent of the capital of the pot for only a 31 per cent chance of taking it. It looks bad. Added to that, you will also have to show your hand. Even if he is on a desperate bluff (and, with only $15 left, he may be) you have to remember that, at the moment, you have no hand. Even if your opponent has only a Pair of 2s, he is still beating you right now.

Open-ended Straight draw offers basic odds of 31.5 per cent of completing the Straight with two cards to come, and 17.4 per cent of success with only one card to come.

Unless it requires only the smallest of bets (or smallest of percentages of the pot), to play for the so-called gut-shot Straight draw – where only one card can help you – is a real amateur move:

You hold   A♦ J♠

and the flop comes   K♣ 10♦ 5♣

Only a queen will give you a good hand and, although you would hold the top Straight, with two clubs on board, you may yet face a Flush – and these are the types of hand that can cost you dearly. You bet good money to stay in, and Q♣ hits the board on the river. It makes your hand but, when you raise, you get re-raised. Are you winning, or has Q♣ just given an opponent his Flush?

Gut-draw Straights (where you require a single card) are VERY poor propositions: 16.5 per cent with two cards to come; a paltry 8.7 per cent with one card to come. Avoid them unless you can stay in the pot very cheaply.

The only advantage of such a draw is that, if you do make your hand, you may well win a sizeable pot because it will be hard for your opponents to read that you were on such a draw.

Similarly, turning 2 Pair into a Full House: 16.5 per cent with two cards to come; 8.7 per cent with only the river to show.

Turning a Pair into Trips is harder still – you need one of only two cards to succeed: 8.4 per cent with two cards to come; 4.3 per cent with one card to come.

As you gain more experience and you learn to judge your opponents' actions with more reliability you will find yourself playing the person as much as the cards in front of you. The world's very best players play like this often – their senses are so fine-tuned, so alert to every nuance of their opponents' behaviour that the importance of the odds can be downgraded as other skills increase. All players, however, should know the key basic drawing odds.

"Pot Committed"
This is a term to describe a hand where there is so much in the pot that not to call the last bet would be foolish. This

often occurs when you are just about all-in (that is to say, the last of your bankroll at the table is in the pot). It is more common in tournament play than in cash play since, in a cash game, your last $5 is just as important as any other $5 you had sitting in front of you and, to that end, it should be invested wisely. In a tournament, if everyone else has $500 in front of them, you hanging around with $5 is unlikely to lead to success, so you might decide to stay in a pot even when the odds don't look so good for you. At least if you win, you're back in the tournament.

You hold

and you decide to raise pre-flop. You're called by one opponent

and the flop comes

with $140 in the pot and only $10 left in your hand, your opponent bets $10 into you. He probably has an ace and has you beaten but, there are ways you can win this hand and then you'll be back in the tournament. You are pot-committed. To fold now, and leave yourself with $10 is almost certainly wrong. So you call and hope for a queen to appear or two clubs. All unlikely but, if it happens, you're back in the tournament.

Occasionally, the same principle will apply when your opponent is short-stacked.

There is $70 in the pot

you hold

and the board shows

no one has made a raise and, for whatever reason, you are still in the pot. Your one opponent now bets his last $4, declaring all-in. Should you bet?

Well, you might as well. Your Pair of 7s is almost certainly not winning, but for $4 into a pot worth $74, why not? After all, if a 7 or an ace hits on the river, you will likely scoop the pot. Referring to our chart of odds again, you have five outs (cards which can help you) with one card to come. That offers you a 10.9 per cent chance of hitting something, yet you are only betting about 6 per cent of the value of the pot.

These situations are further examples of where you need to take just a little more time than usual before you make your decision. I want you to be a player who keeps the odds firmly to the forefront of his mind but also one who realizes that there are times, both statistically and from reading your opponents' behaviour, that to play seemingly against the odds is the right strategy.

7

BANKROLL AND MONEY MANAGEMENT

Your bankroll is the amount of money you have set aside for playing poker. Whatever your financial status, it is very important to keep your bankroll separate from your other money. Apart from protecting your money and ensuring that you can still pay the bills at the end of the month, this should allow you to keep close track of how you are faring. This is very important and is all part of the need to be completely self-aware, even as a social poker player. In order for good players to win, there have to be losers – and there are lots of them. However, losers at poker tend to be delusional: they think they have broken even, or that they are just ahead. A friend of mine who organizes a regular home game, kept track of all eight players' wins and losses for a year and then asked them to assess how they thought they had done. All eight were convinced that they were ahead. In fact, two were well ahead, four were down a little and two were down a lot. If you are losing consistently, then you are in the wrong game, playing with the wrong people for the wrong stake and/or you are just plain lousy. Whatever the reason, to avoid losing, you must make changes.

Setting Your Bankroll
Especially in No-Limit games, there can be huge fluctuations over a short period of time. Your bankroll must be sufficient to cover such downturns when they occur. Since you decide in what games you play, you can limit your losses to the amount which you bring to the table. If your bankroll is, say $1,000 for the year, then to buy-in to a game where you have to start with $200 is a risky venture. You might win and increase your bankroll considerably. But, equally, you might play perfect poker and lose your $200 on the first hand. You pull out another $200 and it could go the same way. You could be wiped out in a few minutes' play.

My advice would be to start with an absolute minimum of twenty times your usual buy-in (so, that's $4,000 if you're going to play in that $200 game). Better still, work on a ratio of fifty times or even one hundred times. In this way, if you hit a run of losing games, you won't feel pressured or depressed and it won't affect the way you play.

Therefore, starting with that $1,000 bankroll, it's time to buy into the game for $20, or maybe $50. That's just fine for a low-limit game, or low-blinded pot limit or no-limit game, say 50c/$1. If you are as good as you think you are, your bankroll will increase irregularly but consistently over time, and you'll be able to buy-in for more, and play in bigger games. However, beware . . .

Choosing Your Game
Poker is about winning. Find a game that you can beat consistently. Then, having increased your bankroll, go up a level – just one level though, because as the stakes increase the average standard of the game will improve.

A friend of mine, who is based in Las Vegas, played in the $10/20 limit game for a year. He managed to triple his bankroll, which was a good size to start with. I felt that he was a strong player. He decided to move up – not to a $20/40 game, the next game up – but to a much higher one. He lost his entire bankroll within three weeks. Dispirited, depressed and broke, he went back to the $10/20 game and slowly worked his way back again. Now, you can see him in the $20/40 game three nights a week at a famous casino in town. He wins regularly and is waiting until he has one hundred times the bankroll he needs to move up, just one level, to the next game.

It's a classic poker expression and you will have heard it before, but it is very important:

If you can't spot the sucker at your table within fifteen minutes – it's you!

Rate yourself honestly at your table and ask yourself whether there are at least two players poorer than you. If there are – that's your game. Learn from the stronger players, pay for your lessons from the weaker ones. It is much, much better to win a little consistently from a modest game, than to try to be dashing and glamorous and sexy at a big-boys' table. Trust me, I know. I've done it, and I've lost it, and my ego is in check. I'm in the medium-sized game secretly wishing I had a million bucks so I could play with the whales. But I don't. If, in many years' time, I get a chance to tangle with the high-rollers, I want to be fit and lean and in with a seriously good chance. That's not to say I haven't played against many good players. That is the beauty of tournaments and satellites – you can still enjoy the glamorous action without the risk to your financial well-being.

Coming and Going

Don't play in a table that has too high stakes or too many strong players. There will be other games to be discovered and other times to play.

Don't leave a table when you're winning – that you are winning is an important advantage to you and it may well intimidate your opponents. However, be aware when the weaker players leave – hopefully cleaned out by you – and you are just left with the stronger ones. That is the time to smile and cash in. The weaker players will be back and that is when you want to sit down again.

The other time to leave the table is easier to spot, but harder to do: when you are tired, upset, emotionally distraught from a series of bad beats or poor cards. Folding hand after hand for hours can be demoralizing, particularly if you can only play from time to time and you've been looking forward to this session during days of tedious, mind-numbing work. Make a colossal effort and rise from the table. Have a coffee, a long cold drink, grab some fresh air – and then head back for a second try. If you still aren't firing – or zigging when you should be zagging – call it a day (or a night).

House Rakes and Charges

In casino and online games, the house takes a fee for managing the game. In a casino, this will pay for the dealers and the cards; online, the operators have to pay for expensive software and, oh yes, make a big profit. When you play a high-stake game, the fees that are charged usually have no impact but, for low-limit games, they can be important.

For example, in some casinos, an hourly fee is charged. In a low-limit game, for four hours' play, this might amount to as much as 20 per cent of your bankroll. That is an edge you will have great difficulty in overcoming and the only winners at the end of the day will be the casino. If that is the case, you will do better finding a group of friends and acquaintances and playing at home. But, remember, you may have to buy chips, baize, cards, etc., and if you are an irregular player, the casino's charges may work out better for you.

Online, and in other card clubs, the house takes a rake from each pot. This is usually 5 per cent of the pot, up to a certain limit. The advantage here is that if you are having a tough time and not doing well, at least you are not also paying out for table fees – the winners are doing that. Also, most rakes do not operate if no flop has been shown. So, if you raise before the flop and no one calls, you get the pot and you get to keep all of it.

There is little you can do about these charges if you want to play online or in a club or casino, but be aware of them and how they may affect your bankroll.

Tipping

Not something to worry about in home games, online games and many European card clubs. However, in Las Vegas and the card clubs throughout the US, most dealers work for minimum wages and rely upon tips from players to earn a half-decent living. In low-limit games, the tradition is for the winner of each pot to tip $1 and, if the pot is very small, to "chop-chop" which offers the dealer 50c. If you say "chop" or "chop-chop", the dealer will understand that you are giving him half the usual tip. In bigger games, you can decide how much to tip the dealer and the high-rollers often wait until the end of the session and then hand over a wad. Traditionally, however, you share your good fortune by tipping a little each time you win a pot.

8

ONLINE POKER

Playing poker online is a great way to start playing the game. You are in your own home, you have a drink by your side (although, contrary to the romantic image, alcohol and winning poker rarely mix), you can have notes to hand, you can even have a more experienced friend talking you through the first few hands and watching your game. It isn't "real" poker, with all the cut and thrust of a live game, but it is a brilliant alternative form of the game.

Play Money or Real Money?
Almost all online poker rooms offer the choice of play money or real money. If you know nothing about the game, by all means play out a few hands with play money until you're familiar with the etiquette, the speed of play, and the style of the game. However, it is with money that you keep score at poker, and using play money simply encourages everyone to stay in the pot until the end. They have, in effect, nothing to lose. For this reason, play money games are not worth your time, and you should abandon them quickly.

Which Site?
There is a huge selection of potential sites run by both well-known companies and new Internet ventures. Many use the same software and simply apply a "skin" which brands the site with corporate logos. The best advice is to talk to friends who play online and get recommendations.

Getting Started
When you first sign up, you register a credit card and download a sum of money into your online account, usually using an online payment processing system such as "PayPal". Whilst it is prudent to ensure that your credit card company covers you for online fraud, there are very few examples of malpractice. Businesses such as Party-Poker.com and Betfair.com/pokerroom are huge international concerns and any problems could damage a reputation for years and destroy a massive money-making business, so security both of your money and of the sites' systems is high quality.

When making your selection, make sure that you get a sign-up bonus. Usually, for your first download, you will get a 50 per cent or 100 per cent bonus, up to approximately £100 or $200. This will be a useful addition to your bankroll while you learn the game. Usually, you are required to play a certain number of hands before receiving your bonus but, if you are planning to play, you would do that anyway.

When you first enter the site, you create a username and nickname. You then enter a "Lobby" area which shows you all the games in progress, from which you choose your stake and select your game or reserve your place. You can then watch games in progress, or play cash games yourself. However, my recommendation would be to seek out the tournament section. On popular and successful sites, you will find tournaments large and small commencing every few minutes twenty-four hours a day. I would recommend entering a ten-player event for a $5 entry fee – that's all you can lose – and see how you get on. See the tournament section for etiquette and strategy.

Once you start making it into the money (usually the last three from ten starters) you can then consider playing in the cash games.

Some sites offer loyalty-style points for playing in games which can then be used to enter so-called "free-roll" events, where the entry fee is paid using these points. These represent a great chance to practise for free and are well worth hunting down.

Making Character Notes
When I first started playing online I immediately set to work on notes for all the players I encountered. Because there are a large number of players, it was hard to remember a player's style and it was useful to be able to reference that information when selecting a table and once playing. My study soon filled up with ring-bound notepads.

Now, on many sites, you can double click, or right-click, on the player's name and you get a little jotter pad on which you can make notes about that player. When you see the players' names at the table, a logo identifies that you have a note on them and you can then look them up. This is hugely useful, but it does tie you to one site since, if you switch sites, your notes don't come with you.

When making notes about each player, I date them, so that I can later see whether a player conforms to the sketch I have made of him. Perhaps the first time I played with him, he was on tilt, or in a bad mood, or licking his wounds . . .? However, I have noticed that players tend to

remain quite consistent to the style in which they play.
You can identify them in any form you like. Phil Helmuth
Jnr – one of the greatest poker players around – recom-
mends thinking of your opponents as animals with different characteristics but, whatever you do, you need to note
their important characteristics: in your opinion, are they
strong, average or weak; tight or loose; a bluffer or a rock;
a fish or a respecter of raises?

For example, I encountered a player a few weeks back
whom I hadn't played against for six months. I saw I had
made a note on him. It told me that he was "timid and never
raised without the best hand; no evidence of a bluff – ever!"
This proved useful because I was the dealer holding:

With the Blinds at $1/2, the player in the position in front
of me raised to $5. I decided to see if he was trying to
steal the Blinds and push me out and I re-raised, making
it $15. The player on whom I had notes called this
re-raise, as did the original raiser. The alarm bells were
ringing . . . This indicated a very strong hand and, from
this player, a very, very strong hand. By now, I was sure
that the timid player had a seriously big hand and that my
hand was probably not winning. The flop came:

With no cards higher than my Pair, this was a great flop
for me, but my timid opponent now bet $25 and was
called by my right-hand opponent. I decided to get out,
right now. Firstly I thought the timid opponent had got
KK or, more likely, AA, and my other opponent seemed
to think that he had something too. To cut a long story
short, timid opponent had got AA, whilst my right-hand

opponent was betting with A♠ J♠ on a Flush draw, which he didn't make. Put simply, my notes saved me money. That is one of the advantages of online poker: you have many references on which you can call – if you're just prepared to take the time to make the notes.

Another example: a player whom I come up against quite regularly, in the $1/2 no-limit Hold 'Em cash game, always bets $8 when he has AA, KK, or QQ. This is bad play of course, since you should always try to mix up your play as much as possible. But, for me, it's a huge help. He never raises to $8 pre-flop without one of these hands (or if he does, I've not spotted it in hour upon hour of play).

Not only can such notes help you to judge the play of your opponents, they can also be used to select your table. Steer clear of the strong, knowledgeable players and pick another table. The beauty of online poker is that there is always another table, so there is no excuse for poor table selection.

There is now computer software which runs alongside your online poker games which rates all the players online, based on their form and successes. There are several versions now available and to have such information about your opponents is hugely beneficial to your chances of good table selection and eventual victory.

Sit Over Weakness
This is a classic poker tip. In general, money moves clockwise around the poker table. This is because if you are to the left of a player, you have position over them (except the Small Blind over the dealer). Therefore, you have a better chance than anybody to judge your opponent to your right. Given a choice – and online you usually are – try to position yourself to the left of the weak player; in other words, sit over him. Now, you are ready to fold, check, raise or re-raise him, once you have seen what he's up to.

There is nothing more frustrating than watching a player giving away chips and you miss out on them all. As well as your cards, your position will prove vital.

Steal Blinds Aggressively

Online play moves quicker than in real life. Consequently, players tend to demonstrate a strange quirk: they are impatient to get into the action and will play many sub-standard hands but, when they get raised, they tend to be, comparatively, more willing to let them go, feeling that they will get a cheap look at a flop some time soon. Almost one third of the online players I have polled admit to playing at more than one table simultaneously (you can play as many tables as your server will allow you to open windows). For this reason, players with moderate hands in the Blinds are less inclined to call a raise on the button or one from the button. In this way, you can pick up more Blinds than you would usually. If you find that you have a very aggressive re-raiser sitting to your left, adjust your strategy, or even move tables but, by and large, Blind stealing is an extra profitable action online.

Bluffing

Players love to bluff online, especially in tournaments. They know that you can't hear their heart pounding or see the pulse in their neck throbbing, so bluffing seems easier.

In cash games, you will find a good deal of bluffing too. My advice in online games is to attack players who have just signed in and arrive at your table, especially if they have sat down without a very big bankroll. These players would hate to lose it all on the first hand so, if the hand is shaping up well, this is a good time to get in there with a nice big bet.

9

TOP TEN TIPS FOR TEXAS HOLD 'EM

These are ten tips for the beginner and for the less experienced player. Many hold good throughout your poker career, but, mainly, they will get you off to a good start. Good players may turn up their noses at one or two but that's just fine. When you get better, you can judge for yourself.

1. There is something to learn from every hand you play
If you want to get good at poker, you must be focused on improving your game. Do not take the results – be they good or bad – of one session to represent your standard. These hands are but a few from a whole lifetime of hands and you may just have been lucky or have suffered a series of bad beats.

Ask yourself whether you think you played the hand correctly; even ask other players what they think. Keep analysing yourself.

Above all, remember that to succeed, you have to be patient and play only decent starting hands. All those hands you do not play must not be wasted. Watch your opponents, note their styles (either mentally, or if online, use a jotter pad or a pen and paper) and learn from their successes and failures. Remember that you have to be aggressive at all times and attack the weak and test the strong with caution. There is no room for sentiment or sympathy. Learn all you can from every hand and then use that information to get straight back at your opponents.

2. Choose your game

Online or live, your choice of game will hugely affect your chances of success. Do not be ambitious to play high-stake poker until you know the game, until you have played many hundreds of hours of poker, until you've read not just this beginners' guide, but a whole series of intermediate and more advanced volumes. Keep in mind that the players in the bigger games would adore to have you join them before you are ready: it would be Christmas come early for them as they take all your chips from you slowly but steadily. And don't be taken in by their plati-tudes, their reassurances that you were just unlucky. They want you there before you are ready and only you can be sensible enough to resist their spider-like entreaties.

Only when you are winning consistently – say 70 per cent of the time – in your current game, should you consider moving up. Make sure that you have the bankroll to support your new lofty ambitions so that a couple of poor sessions won't make you stressed and unhappy and cause you to cease giving your full attention to your fellow players and the cards in your hand.

3. Money moves clockwise, so attack the players immediately to your right

Money tends to move clockwise at the poker table. For this reason, select seats to the left of players you know/

suspect to be weak. Keep raising them, attacking them, bluffing them. If you happen to get re-raised by a player to your left, you can always back down gracefully. The chances are that they have spotted the weakness too and they are after the weaker player's money. Don't be over-generous, but be flexible in letting them take you off the pot from time to time (i.e. fold when they make a raise even if you suspect that they may be bluffing). If you want to talk to players at your table, that's just fine. Charm, flatter, even seduce the players on your left – if you can induce even a micron of sympathy towards you, it may be worth money to you later. Don't be nice to your right-hand opponent or his right-hand opponent. You're after them. You want their chips; all their chips . . .

4. Trust your instincts and don't be afraid to fold the best hand

It is easy to take it personally when you make a bet and someone raises you aggressively. They want you to take it personally, they want to needle you. Worse still is when someone makes a lousy call, and then the river saves his hide, and he gloats about it. Distance yourself from this from the start, because it will happen throughout your poker career and it will never stop. The effect this needling sometimes has is to persuade you to stay in hands longer than you should and to call bets, even when you know, deep down, that you are beaten.

The problem with poker is that there are no prizes for having the second best hand, even if there are still half a dozen players left in the pot. It is far better to lay down the best hand from time to time and lie in wait for when you hold the nuts, than to go chasing close decisions when, perhaps, it all comes down to the kicker. It may make you feel good when you get it right but, especially when you are starting out, you won't get it right that often and it will dent your confidence as well as your bankroll.

If your head is telling you that you are beaten, trust it, and lay down the hand.

The final consideration is this: if you fold the best hand and you see that you would have won (because there is a showdown between other players, for example) no one knows that you laid down the best hand. Play the hand to its conclusion and lose, and everyone sees what you did and they will use that information against you subsequently. In other words, hold your counsel, accept that you are developing your judgment, and start by playing conservatively.

5. With a choice between calling and raising, or checking and betting, always opt for the more aggressive move

If you are not sure whether to bet or check, or call or raise, take the aggressive action. Indeed, if you decide that you really cannot bring yourself to raise, then consider folding and getting out of the hand – you're obviously not that good.

This may seem aggressive for a beginner's tip, but it will get you off to a good start.

It has so many advantages:

(a)   You may force everyone to fold, and win the pot there and then.
(b)   You may persuade your opponent(s) to check on the next round and then you might check yourself and get to see the river card for free.
(c)   You may hit your hand and build an even bigger pot.
(d)   You will give the impression of confidence which is usually lacking from beginners who, typically, call

bets and limp into hands and just hope that something good happens. You are being far more proac-
tive and you will cause things – usually good things –
to happen.

6. Your goal is not to win lots of pots, it is to win lots of money – that is how success is measured at poker

Do not confuse winning lots of pots with being a successful poker player. The only scale on which to measure your
success is how much money you have at the end of the
year. If you are in profit, that's good; if you are hugely in
profit, that's better.

Many players stay in the pot too long and then feel that
they might as well call the last bet just to check that they
haven't won the pot. Staying in until the end will mean
that you win more pots, but it will cost you so much
money that you will turn out a big loser.

7. The time to fold your cards is pre-flop or on the flop

There are games and specific times when you find that
staying in a little longer will pay off. However, for the vast
majority of games, the time to get out of the action is
before you've committed much money to the pot, namely
before the flop and once the flop has been dealt. Being
passionately in love with your Pair of queens when you
have raised and there have been two callers and the flop
comes A K 2 will just cost you money – all your money.
Some love affairs are doomed and, at Texas Hold 'Em,
the flop is the time when you have to decide that you and
your hand are just not meant for one another.

8. Money that you have invested in the pot is gone; it must have no bearing on your future actions
Beginners and weaker players stare longingly at a pot and reflect that they have contributed so much to it that surely it is worth putting in just a little bit more to try to get their money back. This is a disastrous attitude. The fact is, once you have bet into a pot, that money is no longer yours; it has gone and belongs solely to the pot. The only appraisal worth making is this: at this point, is it worth investing the amount required to call an opponent's bet based on your hand, what you think your opponent holds, and what the pot is worth? Who has contributed to that pot is irrelevant.

9. Patience is everything
Poker is NOT a fast-moving, exhilarating, glamorous game. I know that you don't want to hear this and I'm sorry to be the one to break it to you, but it's not. In fact, often, it's quite boring.

When you are in the hand and you have a genuine chance to win the pot, out-think, outplay and outwit your opponents, your adrenalin will be pumping and it feels like the sexiest game there is. However, that is not going to happen very often. The real time when money is won or lost – particularly when you are starting out at the game – is when you first glance at your two hole cards. If you can summon up the self-control to keep folding sub-standard hands, even if that goes on for hours on end – and sometimes it will – then, when you emerge from a session, you'll find that you are a winner.

Most of us go on tilt from time to time, emotions get the better of us and you hear yourself saying: "I know it was a risk, but I've been picking up rubbish all day so I thought I'd give it a go." Those comments accompany the loss of a big part of your carefully preserved bank-roll.

Put simply: if you can be more patient than the other players around the table, you will win. In fact, you'll probably win almost every session you play but you will certainly be a winner at the end of a few sessions because the major weakness of all poker players is lack of patience and self-control. Resolve to be better than most people.

Many online poker rooms offer statistics on your game. Using these, you can study what percentage of hands you are playing, what percentage you are winning, when you fold your cards, and whether you are, predominantly, calling or raising. When you look at these, you want to see that, unless you are enjoying an amazing rush of good cards, you are playing about 10 per cent of hands dealt and that, when you do see the flop, you are winning the majority of those hands. If that is your profile, you will be in profit.

10. Raise when you have the best hand
This is a very simple rule. Many more experienced players will argue that there are many times when it is the wrong advice. However, when you are starting out at poker, you need to build your confidence. Slow-playing a good hand, only to find yourself overtaken on the turn or river, can be utterly demoralizing. In turn, this leads to your feeling that you, somehow, need to get even. So, you start to play sub-standard hands, or stay in the hand for draws that are way against the odds. In other words, being clever (when you're not experienced enough) just leads to trouble. Follow this tip and you may win a little less, but you will win.

In one online poker room there is a player I rate very highly. He only plays the mid-size games ($1/2 and $2/5

Blinds) and he always seems to have more money in front of him than his buy-in. We talked a little about drawing odds online and then chatted by e-mail. He told me simply: in online poker rooms (he only plays online) he makes a solid income by raising with the best hand. He's a good enough player to know that, when he has the nuts, he can slow-play the hand but, otherwise, he keeps it simple. He says he knows he could play differently but, in the games in which he likes to play, he consistently prevails by raising with the best hand. This is the talk of a winner. He's found his game, he knows he can beat it, and he keeps it simple. Perfect.

GLOSSARY

add-on   in a tournament, you may be offered the opportunity to add to your chips by buying extra chips after the first session of play

all-in   to place all your remaining chips into the pot

ante   bet made before the cards are dealt on each hand

bad beat   a hand where you lose to a player against the expected odds

bet   to make the first movement of chips on any betting round

bicycle   nickname for a low Straight (A2345)

big slick   AK "in the hole"

Blind, Blinds   compulsory bets placed before the cards are dealt: Small Blind is placed by the player directly to the left of the dealer; Big Blind (sitting directly to the left of the Small Blind) places bet usually double the size of the Small Blind

bluff   to attempt to steal the pot by
                     representing a hand stronger than the
                     one actually held

board   the table; the community cards
                     showing on the table

boat   nickname for a Full House

burn   to discard; the dealer "burns" the top
                     card before dealing the "flop", "turn"
                     and "river"

button   the dealer button which denotes the
                     position of the dealer; also sometimes
                     referring to the player in that seat

buy-in   the exchange of cash for chips; the
                     amount required to sit at a given table

call   to match the highest bet made to date

cash in   to leave the table, and exchange your
                     chips for cash

check   when no other player has bet, to check
                     is to make no bet at that stage
                     (sometimes indicated by tapping the
                     table)

check-raise   a play that is usually strong. To check
                     at first and then, once an opponent
                     bets, to raise him

chip, chips   also known as "checks", these are
                     circular plastic or clay discs which
                     represent different financial values and
                     which are used instead of cash in
                     almost all poker games

community   the flop, turn and river cards dealt face
cards   up in the middle of the table

cowboys   nickname for kings

dealer	the player who deals (or for whom a paid dealer deals) the deck, before this honour moves on to the next player in a clockwise direction
down cards	your "hole" or "pocket" cards
draw	to improve your hand with the community cards
Draw, 5-card	a variation of poker where you are dealt five cards and then have an opportunity to exchange one or more to improve your hand
early position	the player positions closest to the left of the dealer; the first players to decide what to do
fifth street	the fifth and final community card, also known as "the river"
final table	the last table of ten players (sometimes eight) in a tournament when all other players have been eliminated
fish	a player who stays in pots hoping to catch the right cards to create a winning hand – but against the odds
flop	the first three community cards
Flush	five cards of the same suit
Flush draw	when you have four cards of the same suit and you are hoping that the subsequent card(s) will produce a fifth card to complete the Flush
fold	to throw away, or muck, one's cards
fourth street	the fourth community card, also known as "the turn"
heads up	head-to-head play at a table containing only two players

high-roller   a player who competes for very high stakes

hole cards   the player's two secret cards, dealt face down

hole, in the   as above

home game   poker played at home

house, the   the casino or club in which you are playing

kicker   card or cards not involved in the formation of a poker combination, but still part of the five-card poker hand

late position   player(s) closest to the dealer, almost last to act on each round of the betting

lay down   to concede or give in; often a good play in poker if you feel that you are beaten

limp in   to call a small bet in "late position" when you are unlikely to be raised

loose   a loose player is likely to play too many hands, remain in pots for too long and make speculative plays which will result in chips being lost

mid-position   in the middle of the table between the Big Blind and the dealer

muck   to fold, or discard

no-limit   a game with no maximum limits on the amount which can be bet

nut, nuts   the best possible hand; a "Nut" Flush would be an ace-high Flush, with no chance of a Straight Flush for any other player

out, outs	card or cards which will complete your hand and improve it, usually to winning status
overcard(s)	higher card(s): the cards in your hand are overcards if they are higher than those showing in the community cards; alternatively, the flop can produce overcards which are higher than those in your hand
overpair	higher Pair
pocket rockets	AA "in the hole"
position	a player's location at the table, measured in terms of the order in which action must be taken on each round of the betting
pot	the collection of chips (sometimes cash) which will be awarded to the winner of the hand
raise	increase the size of the biggest bet at the table
re-buy	in a tournament, when you lose all your chips early on, you may be offered the opportunity to pay the entry fee again for another chance and another set of starting chips
re-raise	as above, once a player has already raised; considered a very strong, intimidating move
river	the fifth and final community card sometimes known as "fifth street"
rock	a player who chooses only the best hands to enter the action and bets only when he is sure that he is best

rush	a roll, a sequence of successful plays
satellite	a qualifying event for a big poker tournament
school	a poker school; a regular poker game where you never stop learning . . .
second Pair	a Pair formed by the second highest card on the board and one in your hand
set	3 of a Kind, "Trips"
short stack	when you have less than the average amount of chips in front of you
shorthanded	a poker game containing four players or fewer; the value of hands often changes as a result of having fewer players at the table
showdown	when a bet (or bets) is called after the river card, all players must show their hole cards; the best hand wins
side pot	a secondary (sometimes tertiary) pot, formed because one player is all-in and cannot bet any more into the pot, contested by the remaining players
slow-rolling	to turn over a winning hand slowly after another player believes that he has won; poor form at the poker table
slowplay	to give the impression of weakness or uncertainty by checking or calling bets rather than raising them
Small Blind	See Blind, Blinds
Straight	five cards of mixed suits in sequence
Stud, 5-card	an old variation of poker where you are dealt five cards and there is then betting. Not popular these days

suited of the same suit

tell an indication, often subconscious or unrecognised by the player himself, by which other players may gain an insight into the strength of a player's hand

tilt, on tilt usually a sign of frustration or anger, a player may go "on tilt" by playing too many hands of poor quality and subsequently showering opponents with chips

top Pair A Pair formed by the highest card on the board and one in your hand

Trips a "set"; 3 of a Kind

turn the fourth community card; sometimes known as "fourth street"

whale a gambler or poker player of enormous wealth for whom big losses scarcely register

WSOP the World Series of Poker – the World Championships of the game, held each May and June in Las Vegas

INDEX

A

Aces high, 28
Add-on, 119
'All-in', 22, 119
Ante, 76, 119

B

Bad beat, 87–89, 119
Bankroll, 99–100
Bet, to, 26, 119
Betting, 31–32
Bicycle, the, 28
Big Blind, 21
  Slick, 41, 119
Blind, Big, 21, 119
  levels, 69
  , Small, 21, 119
Bluff, 19, 46, 57–58, 70, 110,
  119
Board, paired, 54–56
  , the, 26, 119
Boat, 120
'Burns', 25, 120
Button, dealer, 20
  , on the, 45–46
  raise, 45–46
Buy-in, the, 34–35, 120

C

Call, 23, 46–47, 120
Caller, 32
Cash games, 13, 39 *et seq.*, 69
  in, 120
Casino games, 34
Character notes, 107–109
Check, 24, 120
  -raise, 63, 120
Chip and a chair, 73
  counts, 75–76
Chips, 12, 20, 25, 31, 120
Chop/chop-chop, 103
Club games, 34
'Coffee-house', 59
Community cards, 15, 120
Cowboys, 121
'Cut', 21

D

Dealer, 20–21, 45–46, 121
  button, 20
Deck, 9
Down cards, 121
Draw, 121

E

Early position, 121
Emotions, 63–64

F
Fifth street, 16, 121
Final Table, 12, 76–77, 121
Fish/fishes, 47, 121
5-Card Draw, 11, 121
  Stud, 9, 11, 124
Flop, the, 15, 49 et seq., 121
  pairing, 54–56
Flush, 121
  draw, 94, 121
  , Nut, 17, 28
  , Royal, 10
  , Straight, 10
Fold, 9, 21–22, 23, 121
4 of a Kind, 10
Fourth street, 16, 121
Full House, 10

H
Hands not to play, 43–44
'Head to head', 20, 77
Heads Up, 77, 122
High Card, 10
  roller, 122
  Straight, 28
Hole cards, 15, 122
  , in the, 122
Home games, 33, 122
Honour card, 43
House charges/rakes, 102–103
  , the, 122

K
Kickers, 29, 122

L
Lay down, 122
Limit poker, 35
Limp in, 122
'Lock' on the hand, 58
Loose player, 122

M
Money, play, 105
Muck, 21–22, 122

N
No-limit poker, 36, 122
Nut Flush, 17, 28
  Straight, 17, 28
Nuts, 28, 58–60, 122

O
Odds, pot, 74, 93 et seq.
1 Pair, 10
Online games, 33–34, 105 et
   seq.
'Out', an, 93, 123
  cards, 93
Outdrawn, 19
Overcards, 56, 123
Overpair, 51–53, 123

P
Pack, 9
Pairs, lower, 56
  , premium, 41
Pass, 23
Patience, 39, 116–117
Percentages, 92
Perfect tie, 29–30
Play money, 105
Pocket rockets, 41, 123
Position at the table, 44–45,
   109, 123
  , late, 80, 122
  , mid, 122
Pot, 25, 123
  committed, 96–98
  limit, 35
  odds, 74, 93 et seq.
  , side, 30–31
Premium pairs, 41, 46

R

Raise, 23, 46–49, 57–58, 123
  , button, 45–46
Re-buy, 123
Re-raise, 24, 123
River, the, 16, 60–63, 123
Rock, 123
Royal Flush, 10
Rush, 123

S

Satellites, 68, 123
School, poker, 124
Second Pair, 53–54, 124
Set, 124
Short-handed games, 77, 124
  -stacked, 72, 73, 124
Showdown, 9, 16, 32, 124
Side pots, 30–31, 36, 124
Sit over weakness, 109–110
Slow-rolling, 32, 124
Slowplay, 124
Small Blind, 21, 124
Starting hands, 41–42, 64–65,
    77 *et seq.*

Straight, 10, 124
  draw, open-ended, 95
  Flush, 10
  , gut-draw, 96
  , High, 28
  , Nut, 17, 28
Suited-almost connectors, 78
  connectors, 43–44, 78

T

Take-down option, 36
Tells, 81 *et seq.*, 125
3 of a Kind, 10, 124
Tie, perfect, 29–30
Tilt, on, 40–41, 125
Tipping, 103
Top Pair, 125
Tournaments, 37, 67 *et seq.*
Trips, 27, 124, 125
Turn, the, 16, 60–62, 125
2 Pair, 10

W

Whale, 125
Wheel, the, 28
World Series of Poker, 13, 34,
    125